D1497956

The Cornish Ordinalia

Religion and Dramaturgy

The Cornish Ordinalia

Religion and Dramaturgy

ROBERT LONGSWORTH

HARVARD UNIVERSITY PRESS
CAMBRIDGE, MASSACHUSETTS 1967

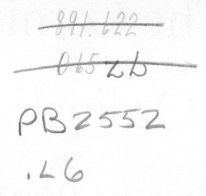

PB 2552

.L 6

© Copyright 1967 by the President and Fellows of Harvard College
All rights reserved
Publication of this book has been aided by a grant from the Hyder Edward
Rollins Fund

Distributed in Great Britain by Oxford University Press, London
Library of Congress Catalog Card Number 67-22869
Printed in the United States of America

TO CAROL

In world nis non so wyter mon
That al hire bounte telle con.

DEC 17 1968

DEC 17 1986

Contents

Preface

A PREFACE is apt to be an equal mixture of apology and acknowledgment. This poor waif of a study has been so often the target of a colleague's wit or of a student's wonder that I am not inclined to render it further service by indulging in apology. The task of acknowledging my obligations is much more welcome and much more urgent.

My debt to scholars who have labored over and commented on the subjects that interest me here is everywhere apparent in these pages. Less apparent, but no less helpful, is the counsel of teachers and advisers who by their wisdom have generously mitigated my ignorance. Professors Morton W. Bloomfield, Charles Dunn, and B. J. Whiting graciously guided this study in its earliest form as a Ph.D. dissertation in English at Harvard. The work has greatly profited by friendly suggestions from Professor David C. Fowler, Professor Robert A. Fowkes, James A. Devereux, S.J., and Professor Andrew Bongiorno.

Professor Thomas Jones cordially arranged for me to spend a happy winter in study at the University of Wales, where J. R. F. Piette put at my disposal his considerable learning, patience, counsel, and good humor as a tutor in Cornish. H. L. Douch, Curator of the County Museum of Cornwall, kindly gave me access to the very helpful though lamentably unpublished manuscripts in the Morton Nance Bequest, which is now deposited in the library of the Museum. I am grateful to the Royal Institution of

Cornwall for permission to quote from that material, and to the Mediaeval Academy of America for permission to quote from the translation by Roy J. Deferrari of Hugh of St. Victor, *On the Sacraments of the Christian Faith.*

Furthermore, I have enjoyed the hospitality and services of the Harvard College Library, the National Library of Wales, the British Museum, and the Bodleian Library. I have had the benefit of knowledgeable technical advice from John Boe, Malcolm Parkes of Keble College, Oxford, and Richard Rouse, formerly of the Harvard Library. With such appreciable help as I have had, I hardly need note what is obvious—that whatever errors remain are my own.

I am happy here to express my gratitude for material aid and encouragement, at various stages of this work, to the Danforth Foundation, to the Committee on General Scholarships of Harvard University, and to Oberlin College. To many friends and colleagues I am indebted in various ways for encouragement and advice, and that sense of obligation is not diminished by my failure to name them all here. After all, the name that ought to be most conspicuous among my acknowledgments is itself, though of necessity, absent. I have come to respect and admire the anonymous author of the *Ordinalia,* and my most devout wish is that this study will have done him justice.

Oberlin
February 22, 1967

The Cornish Ordinalia

Religion and Dramaturgy

Abbreviations Used in Citations

EETS: The Early English Text Society
OM: De Origine Mundi, first part of the *Ordinalia*
PC: Passio Domini Nostri Jhesu Christi, second part of the *Ordinalia*
PG: J. P. Migne, ed. *Patrologiae Cursus Completus.* Series Graeca
PL: J. P. Migne, ed. *Patrologiae Cursus Completus.* Series Latina
RD: De Resurrexione Domini, third part of the *Ordinalia*

I. Introduction

OF ALL THE VERNACULAR DRAMATIC CYCLES that probably existed
in England during the Middle Ages, only five are extant. Four of
these works, which treated in a more or less episodic fashion the
spiritual history of man from the Creation to the Last Judgment,
have received widespread scholarly attention. The fifth survives
not, like the others, in English, but in the Cornish language. This
Ordinalia, as the cycle is called, has been ignored by some writers
and dismissed by others as either unimportant or uninteresting.
The Cornish vernacular in which it is written, a little-known mem-
ber of the Brythonic strain in the Celtic family of languages, has
no doubt been a considerable obstacle to students of the drama,[1]
for Cornish died out, according to the most popular account, with
the last venture into sobriety of the celebrated fishwife of Mouse-
hole, Mrs. Dolly Pentreath, in about 1777. Furthermore, apart
from the *Ordinalia,* the Cornish literary remains are unhappily
few.[2]

Even the few scholars who have dealt with the Cornish
Ordinalia have given it short shrift. Their comments, in fact, savor
more of wistfulness than of authority. Anatole Le Braz, for ex-
ample, in his *Le Théâtre celtique,* quoted with approval Edwin
Norris' remark that the plays "are clearly exotics transplanted from
English soil,"[3] and argued that "The Cornish plays recall similar
English works, and not in name alone: the subjects of both are
also the same, and are presented in the same way, with the same

basic episodes arranged in the same order. The imitation is obvious." [4] Gustave Cohen goes even further: he thinks that "the Cornish drama . . . is but a transposition of the English 'pageants.' " [5] This point of view is remarkably wrongheaded. The *Ordinalia* is certainly not derived from, and is apparently uninfluenced by, any of the surviving plays in English. None of these scholars adduces any evidence for such sweeping assertions beyond Le Braz's worthless comparisons, the vague expansiveness of which might easily be used to prove that the *Ordinalia* was an imitation of virtually any of its dramatic contemporaries.

Hardin Craig even more startlingly and unaccountably suggests that the cycle "was probably derived from similar plays in Brittany." [6] The suggestion is misleading, for it is, however inspired, simply a guess. The earliest extant Breton cycle is, after all, dated considerably later than the *Ordinalia*. Such imaginary bridges cannot be permitted to carry so much traffic. [7] The hasty attribution of imitative and derivative characteristics to the *Ordinalia* has done responsible scholarship a disservice. A more welcome attitude is that of the eminent Cornish scholar Henry Jenner, who cautiously called the work "just the contemporary drama of Christendom, in its local form." [8]

This literary Knossos has, in fact, yielded fewer parallels and borrowings than its miners would like to admit. No dramatic sources have been found. The enigma speaks as darkly as ever.

In a less sweeping fashion, other writers have sought to establish a link between the *Ordinalia* and English vernacular writings, perhaps because brief snatches of English—usually in the form of expletives—occur so often in the drama. Both the *Northern Passion* [9] and the *Southern Passion*,[10] for example, have been mentioned as likely sources for certain scenes and ideas.[11] The notion that the Cornish dramatist may have been familiar with English vernacular writings is, to be sure, attractive. It is also quite possible. On the other hand, to locate within the common repositories of Christianity ideas or characteristic turns that are distinctively English, or in any sense local, is often a trouble-some, even if occasionally a necessary, task. The Christian world of the fourteenth century was probably divided more strongly on issues of faith than on matters of manners and customs. A funda-mental issue, then, is the determination not of the national but of the doctrinal affinities and divergences in the drama.

In order to pursue these ends and to prepare for the study that follows, a few preliminary considerations are in order, so that the Cornish drama may be seen in some perspective. Of all the problems that assail the student, none is more fundamental, as I have suggested, than the unhappy fate that overtook the language itself.

"In Cornwall is two speches; the one is naughty Englyshe, and the other is Cornyshe speche. And there be many men and women the whiche cannot speake one worde of Englyshe, but all Cornyshe": so Andrew Borde, in his celebrated travelogue written about the middle of the sixteenth century.[12] Little more than fifty years afterward Richard Carew could write that "the principal love and knowledge of this language lived in Dr. Kenall the civilian, and with him lieth buried, for the English speech doth still encroach upon it and hath driven the same into the uttermost skirts of the shire. Most of the inhabitants can speak no word of Cornish but very few are ignorant of the English." [13] By 1678 William Scawen, an eminent Cornishman, was pronouncing an obituary: "It may I confess bee lamented, and heavily laid to the charge of us, our Ancestors, and former Progenitors, to have bin too much wanting to our Selves in the loss of the Cornish Speech." [14]

Wherever the responsibility may have lain, it is certain that the Cornish tongue became virtually extinct, so that throughout most of the eighteenth and half of the nineteenth centuries it was of interest only as a curiosity and a matter of concern for solitaries and antiquaries like Daines Barrington, whose discovery of old Dolly Pentreath, communicated to John Lloyd in a letter in 1773, was the object of a satiric effort by "Peter Pindar":

> Hail Mousehole! birth-place of Old Doll. Pentreath,
>   The *last* who jabber'd Cornish—so says Daines,
> Who bat-like haunted ruins, lane, and heath,
>   With Will o' Wisp, to brighten up his brains.[15]

The reasons commonly used to explain the disappearance of the language rather obscure than clarify the causes of its death. The bewildered historian can perhaps find comfort in, though he cannot condone, William Scawen's irascible suggestion that "a general stupidity may be observed to be in the whole county." [16] More seriously, and more to the point, he may emphasize the probable effect on this westernmost county of the burgeoning spirit of commerce in the reign of Elizabeth. Nationalistic fervor in England, the development of a powerful navy for which the harbors of Cornwall were important, and the English war with Spain, in which the county's strategic location may at once be seen to be significant, were no doubt major causes contributing to the spread of English and the diminution of Cornish.[17] These events, at any rate, and the Elizabethan age of which they were characteristics, fall between the comments of Andrew Borde and Richard Carew, and may help to explain the drastic change, there reflected, which saw a living speech wither and die.

These explanations are not fully satisfactory, however, and historians have often felt drawn to add to them the manifest poverty of the Cornish literary tradition.[18] The paucity of documents written in the vernacular is all too evident; nevertheless as late as 1611 a scribe set down a considerable dramatic work in Cornish: in that year, William Jordan, whether as author or copyist, put his name to the colophon of *Gwryans an Bys,* or the *Creation of the World,* a work modeled at least in part on the *Ordinalia.*[19] If there was in Cornwall—and we have no reason for doubt—a strong and lively oral usage of the vernacular, it might have been expected to have sustained the language longer than it did, had not the commercial and English nationalistic enterprises done their work so well. Nonetheless, Scawen deserves to be heard when he pleads that a major reason for the decay of Cornish is the giving over of the Guirremears [*gwary myrs,* or "miracle plays"], which were used at the great conventions of the people, at which they had famous interludes celebrated with great preparations, and not without shews of devotion in them, solemnized in open and spacious downs of great capacity, encompassed about with earthen banks, and in some part stone work of largeness to contain thousands, the shapes of which remain in many places at this day, though the use of them long since gone. These were frequently used in most parts of the county, at the conveniency of the people, for their meeting together, in which they represented, by grave actings, scriptural histories, personating patriarchs, princes, and other persons; and with great oratory pronounced their harangue, framed by art, and composed with heroic stile . . . This was a great means to keep in use the tongue with delight and admiration, and it continued also friendship and good correspondency in the people.[20]

Scawen's nostalgic lament for the language of his country is a fitting introduction to this scrutiny of the most imposing of the surviving representations, the *Ordinalia*.

The *Ordinalia* survives in a single manuscript in the Bodleian Library, Bodl. MS. 791. There are at least two copies of the original manuscript, one by John Keigwyn in the Bodleian Library (Bodl. MSS. 28556–28557), and another apparently by Edward Lhuyd in the National Library of Wales (Peniarth MS. 428E).

The base manuscript itself consists of eighty-three folios of text on parchment, and gives evidence of having had an interesting scribal history in its own right. Fundamentally, the manuscript is the work of two scribes. One hand carries the *Ordinalia* through some 2824 lines devoted to Old Testament events. The second hand picks up the work by adding an envoy to the audience which announces that the first day's play is concluded and instructs the hearers to return on the morrow (*avorow devg a dermyn: OM* 2843); this second scribal hand continues to the end of the drama. At least two and probably more than two scribes have, apparently at some considerably later time, gone through the entire manuscript, making corrections in the text and adding to existing stage directions as well as inserting new directions by way of amplification.[21] The early hands appear to date from the fifteenth century; [22] the later additions are more difficult to place.

The provenience of the *Ordinalia* has by nearly every writer interested in the matter been agreed to be Penryn. The basis for this consensus is almost wholly the evidence of the place names in the *Ordinalia,* together with the convenient presence in Penryn of the ancient foundation of a college of secular canons. Some notes appended by E. Hoblyn Pedler to Norris' edition of the dramas [23] contain the earliest expression of this idea.

No evidence has been presented to indicate with certainty that the *Ordinalia* was ever performed, although a sufficient body of supportive evidence exists to justify the conjecture that it was indeed performed, and in Cornwall; whether by the canons of the collegiate establishment at Glasney and whether in the area of Penryn is a much more conjectural matter. That plays were presented and well attended in Cornwall we have the anecdotal testimony of Richard Carew: "To delight the mind, the Cornish men have gwary miracles . . . in English, a miracle play, [which] is a kind of interlude, compiled in Cornish out of some scripture history, with that grossness which accompanied the Roman's *vetus comedia.* For representing it, they raise an earthen amphitheatre in some open field, having the diameter of his enclosed plain some forty or fifty foot." [24]

At least two earthen amphitheaters of the kind that Carew mentions remain in Cornwall to this day, though both are situated well to the west of Penryn and close to the extremity of Cornwall, at St. Just and near Perranzabuloe. Then, too, Carew's testimony comes more than a century after the latest possible date for the manuscript of the *Ordinalia;* indeed, the "gwary miracles" of which he writes were probably more similar to the *Creation of the World* (*Gwryans an Bys*) than to the *Ordinalia,* and even though the later play was evidently based on the earlier, it is substantially different. Yet Charles Thomas has recently suggested that the remodeling apparent in the henge at Castilly in eastern Cornwall, dating perhaps from the late thirteenth century, may have had as its purpose the erection of a *plen an gwary* similar to those of which Carew spoke.[25] This suggestion certainly encourages, though it does not secure, the assumption of a widespread and enduring tradition of popular dramatic representation in Cornwall.

The lack of conclusive evidence about the production of the *Ordinalia* greatly inhibits the attempt accurately to date the origins of the drama. Although a favorite guess has been the fourteenth century, very little evidence has been adduced to support the supposition, or to fix the date more firmly and precisely.[26]

The best and most serious attempt to arrive at an informed opinion in this matter is that of David C. Fowler, who examines first the form of the place names in the drama, secondly the relationship of the drama to the medieval Cornish passion poem *Pascon Agan Arluth,* and finally the squibs of English that are to be found scattered throughout the text, and on the basis of his analysis of these several matters concludes that "the evidence thus far considered points to the third quarter of the fourteenth century as the period in which to place the composition" of the *Ordinalia.*[27] While Fowler's labors provide a useful basis for a nearer assumption about the date, the *caveat* must be entered that the evidence is extraordinarily tenuous and offers less ground for an accurate supposition than his conclusions may suggest. For example, of the twenty-three place names recorded in the *Ordinalia,* only "seven offer possible evidence for dating the text" and their evidence is highly disputable, as Fowler notes.[28] Indeed, it was on the basis of his own researches, though earlier and less reliable than Fowler's, into the place-name evidence that Pedler fixed on a date in the late thirteenth century.[29]

Furthermore, evidence concerning the relationship of the *Ordinalia* to the poem *Pascon Agan Arluth* rests largely on the equally uncertain proposal that the poem can be dated in the late fourteenth century.[30] Of more interest is Fowler's suggestion, which has sounder support from the texts than his efforts at dating, that the poem is based on the drama. Students have tended, on the basis of no very carefully argued reasons, to regard the obligation as due in the other direction, an assumption from which Fowler enters a serious and competent dissent on the basis of a selective comparison of the texts.[31]

Lastly, the only evidence for dating that Fowler adduces from the usage of Middle English forms is the occurrence of the final *e* when pronounced. The validity of his conclusions here, as he points out, depends greatly on the disputatious and unsettled scholarly problem of when the final *e* ceased to be pronounced in English— and, in the case of these plays, in a highly colloquial English spoken far from London.[32]

Although we may accept Fowler's work as a useful beginning to the study of the problem, his conclusions remain too tentative to provide a basis for a serious assumption about the date of the origin of the *Ordinalia,* and for present purposes it therefore seems advisable to incline toward caution: Chambers' generous attribution of the drama to the fourteenth century is perhaps as secure an assumption as the scholar is warranted to make.

The problems that beset an attempt to date the *Ordinalia* are, furthermore, obstacles to a study of the Cornish language that the drama exemplifies. Historical evidence about the evolution of the language is virtually nonexistent. As Henry Jenner, to whom every student of Cornish is profoundly indebted, remarks, "until the time of Henry VIII. we have no trustworthy information about the state or extent of the language." [33] The only example of Cornish that seems both appreciably earlier than the drama and sufficiently extensive to permit any comparison is a brief vocabulary that survives in British Museum MS. Cotton Vespasian A. xiv. Norris, who prints the vocabulary in full as an appendix, remarks that it "was probably intended rather to explain Latin words to Cornish men than used as a Cornish dictionary." [34] The manuscript is a late twelfth century copy of an original that can be dated about A.D. 1100 and is itself based on Aelfric's Anglo-Saxon glossary.[35] It has been of some value to the philologists, etymologists, and lexicographers who have worked with the language, although it cannot provide the solid ground that one desires.

The history of the linguistic scholarship which has recovered the Cornish language for students can only be mentioned here in passing, interesting though it is. The study of the language may be said to have begun most notably with Edward Lhuyd, celebrated Welshman and keeper of the Ashmolean Museum, whose *Archaeologia Britannica* was conceived as a compendious survey of Celtic antiquities, although only a single volume, dealing with the languages, was published, and that in 1707. He apparently received a great deal of help from a Cornishman, John Keigwyn, who has left transcriptions and translations of the *Ordinalia*. In the mid-nineteenth century, as I have noted, the *Ordinalia* was translated and published by Edwin Norris; at about the same time Whitley Stokes, an eminent Celtic scholar, published the other surviving Cornish plays and the passion poem.[36] Foremost among recent scholars have been Henry Jenner, whose *Handbook of the Cornish Language* is standard, and R. Morton Nance, whose *New Cornish English Dictionary*[37] represents the fruit of a lifetime of labor on the language, and who, together with A. S. D. Smith ("Caradar"), prepared editions and translations of the main body of Cornish literary remains before his death, although for the most part his work is unpublished.

The literary characteristics of the *Ordinalia* cannot be called distinguished. The language is straightforward and unadorned. Figures are rare and, when they do occur, rather uninspired: for example, when Aaron observes of the three rods that are to become the wood of the cross that they have a distinctive savor, he merely remarks that

> A losowys ol a'n bys
> Mar whek smyllyng my a grys
> Ny thothe bys venary.

(From all the herbs of the world such sweet smelling, I believe, will not come for ever: *OM* 1742–1744.) Even the psalmist's speech is simple and plain. King David's apostrophe to his beloved Bathsheba is an unimaginatively hyperbolic "Bersabe flour ol an bys"

(Bathsheba, flower of all the world: *OM* 2121). Indeed, what grace the poetry has derives mainly from its simplicity:

> Cosel my re bowesas
> Assyw whek an hun myttyn
> Gorthyys re bo dev an tas.

(I have rested softly; sweet is the morning sleep. Honored be God the Father: *OM* 2073–2075.) This series of swift, simple declarations has the tranquil beauty of a litany. The language is seldom so supple and poised as in these lines, but it is never more pretentious. Stock phrases, or *chevilles,* like "dev an tas" here, or "mur the ras" (great thy grace), or "gwyn an bys" (white the world— that is, happy), are abundant.[38]

It remains to be noted that the dramas are rather strictly versified throughout. The verses are organized in stanzas, and since most of the speeches can be measured more by stanzas than by lines,[39] the versification generally tends rather to inflate the economy of speech. Swift movements of dialogue, such as the affecting exchange between Abraham and Isaac (*OM* 1305–1394), are exceptional. The dramatist employs, in the main, a seven-syllable line in which, as Norris observes, "the number of syllables is adhered to as strictly as in the syllabic rhythm of Pope and his imitators." [40]

The prosodic qualities of the *Ordinalia* await the scrutiny of a qualified scholar. Loth has described the variety of metrics and of rhyme schemes to be found in the surviving Cornish poetry, but he points out some of the obstacles to a sure prosodic analysis: after all, like Breton, the language and its literary traditions came under the influence of other tongues, and, furthermore, the surviving texts are of a relatively late date.[41] The regularity and seeming simplicity of the syllabification and rhyme read to the ear trained in English verse rather like the "rym dogerel" that Harry Bailly found in Chaucer's *Tale of Sir Thopas,* but the Celtic tradition is in any adequate treatment of the verse more to be reckoned with than misleading English analogues would allow.[42] The most distinctively Celtic characteristic in the verse of the *Ordinalia* is the use of a careful and regular syllabic count.

The *Ordinalia* was designed for presentation on three successive days, and each day's play runs to around three thousand lines of verse, although the third day calls for the longest dramatic effort. At the conclusion of each performance, the most authoritative figure in that day's drama dismisses the audience and, after the first two days, asks for music and celebrating as he bids the hearers to return on the morrow. Corpus Christi is the festival usually associated with the presentation of the medieval cycles, but there are problems that stand in the way of taking it as the obvious occasion for the production of the *Ordinalia*. One problem is the lack of suitable information regarding the celebration of the festival in Cornwall. After all, as a church festival, Corpus Christi developed fairly late; it was not initiated until 1264 and became widely observed only in the fourteenth century. The difficulty of dating the cycle therefore complicates this question, as well. Secondly, the three days of the play would seem less fitted to the one-day Feast of Corpus Christi than, say, either to the three Ember Days preceding Whitsun or to the three "minor" Rogation Days immediately preceding the celebration of the Ascension. Although all these occasions come in the late spring and early summer, it is worthwhile at least to distinguish between them as likely candidates.

Ember Days were days of fasting and prayer, and are somewhat unlikely to have been very carnivalesque, although there is evidence that plays were presented during Whitsuntide at Chester and Norwich.[43] The minor Rogation Days—the Monday, Tuesday, and Wednesday before the festival of the Ascension on Thursday—were also days of fasting and prayer, but they included processions with litanies and were connected with intercessions for a bountiful harvest. They may have been somewhat more festive than the Ember Days before Whitsuntide, since the Rogation processions were significant enough to have been suppressed in 1547. The Ascension is the event in which the *Ordinalia* dramatically culminates, and its commemorative feast would have been especially appropriate as an occasion for the presentation of this drama. On the other hand, inasmuch as the drama is as a whole concerned with the passion and resurrection of Christ, and to the extent that it may be exemplary or illustrative of the sacrifice of the Mass, it is likewise thematically appropriate for the Feast of Corpus Christi, which was conceived in celebration of the mystery of the Holy Eucharist. The problem of fixing on a likely occasion is not urgent, and any proposed solution is speculative. Indeed, any of these church festivals, as well as certain others, would have been appropriate for the presentation of the *Ordinalia*.

If the matter of when the drama was presented is uncertain, a few more shreds of evidence are available for considering how it may have been presented. As I have pointed out, there still exist in Cornwall ancient circular earthworks, or rounds, that were certainly used as rudimentary wrestling rings and are particularly adaptable to the requirements of the *Ordinalia* and the other surviving Cornish dramas. The list of *dramatis personae* at the end of each day's play is followed by a cartographic representation of a circle around the perimeter of which are designated the positions, or *sedes,* as they were probably called, of the chief characters. This evidence of an early theater in the round has been amply discussed elsewhere,[44] and it is sufficient for the present study simply to note that if and when it was presented, the *Ordinalia* had for the purposes of staging to depend on an open circle surrounded on all sides, as one may assume, by spectators, and not on the exigencies of a pageant wagon or a stage shelf.

Another interesting dramatic problem, so far as the staging is concerned, is the large number of performers required. The lists of characters provided in the plays suggest the logistics involved in mounting a performance of the *Ordinalia*. For the first day 56 characters are listed; for the second day, 62, of which at least 47 have not appeared previously; for the third day, 60, of which at least 22 are new. For the three days of the play, then, 125 different characters are listed. In a remote and rural area like Cornwall, whenever the plays may have been presented, there must have been a considerable amount of "doubling"—where one actor would play several parts—and it is likely that some actors not only played a different part on each of the successive days, but also played more than one part within each day's play. That some such doubling actually took place, a stage direction in the Cornish saint's life or miracle play *Bewnans Meriasek* witnesses: "And John ergudyn aredy a horse bakke yt was ye Justis wt constantyn ffor to play ye marchont." [45]

No matter how extensive this "doubling" may have been in the production of the *Ordinalia,* it is well to recognize that three consecutive days of drama, with the variety of characterization and scenic effect that was demanded, would certainly have amounted to an event of major theatrical importance and must have taxed considerably the imaginative and dramatic resources available in Cornwall in the fourteenth and fifteenth centuries. One can only marvel that so little evidence of its presentation remains.

Unfortunately, the matter of stagecraft has been so little dealt with, and information about the subject is so scant, that any remarks made or conclusions drawn, however tempting in the study, are apt to turn swiftly aerial, lacking as they do the safe ballast of fact or knowledge. Such a temptation apparently could overwhelm even so sedate a scholar as Edwin Norris. Despite—or perhaps as revenge for—his painstaking labors with the Cornish language, he could not forebear the comment that the spectacle of the plays actually being presented must have been "more like what we hear of the so-called religious revivals in America, than of anything witnessed in more sober Europe." [46] Although such a remark is amusing today, it reflects a fairly common tendency to see in what one supposes to be the matter of the play a pattern to inform one's notions about the manner of its presentation. When Norris saw in the *Ordinalia* a deficiency of European sobriety—perhaps of his contemporary's "high seriousness"—he was practicing literary criticism, although for the most part he eschewed what must have seemed to so eminent a linguist trifling frivolity.

Since, however, the *Ordinalia* was written to be performed, and since it represents a considerable dramatic and literary effort in a language without, so far as we know, a literary tradition and in a peripheral county where full-bodied theater might not be expected to have flourished, it justly deserves to be studied carefully and closely both as drama and as literature. In order to do so, the student must disengage himself, at least initially, from many dramaturgical expectations that may suit the contemporary theater but would not have suited the medieval theater. The *Ordinalia,* like the other biblical cycles, not only anticipated an audience of believers but also intended to work upon and through their belief.

A case in point may be the considerable variety of incidents dramatized. To the modern eye this apparent turbulence is one of the chief obstacles in the way of an appreciation of the work. The *Ordinalia* endeavors to compass a series of events from the creation of the world to the ascension of Christ. Although the trial and the crucifixion are presented at length and with considerable dramatic articulation, in the main the episodes follow on one another awkwardly and the attempt to manage so compressed a sequence of events threatens often to bring the drama into chaos. A few mitigating forces may, to be sure, be seen at work. In the Old Testament play (*Origo Mundi*), for example, the violent and swift succession of patriarchs, kings, prophets, and their scenic anecdotes is given at least the semblance of unity by the use of the legend of the cross as a thematic thread. In the Passion and Resurrection plays, Christ himself is the center that provides the requisite thematic focus, and, at least dramatically, the "wood of the cross" may be regarded as a kind of surrogate for or type of Christ when it deals with preparatory, prechristian events. Yet to comprehend such patterns, the critic must comprehend the way in which belief itself was ordered.

The variety of incidents treated in the *Ordinalia* is, in fact, understandable, and it is in part the aim of this study to attempt to clarify such understanding, for the *Ordinalia* may be seen as a compression and fusion of the disparate liturgical and ecclesiastical and scriptural experiences that loosely may be associated with the church year and with the symbolic manifestation of church dogma and doctrine. The roots of the *Ordinalia,* as of all the medieval cycles, reach back into the early liturgical elaborations and amplifications of the church: the "literary embellishments, from which the first dramatic representations arose, were inserted into the liturgy for the serious purpose of adornment and exposition, and they were eventually dramatized in a manifest desire to convey edifying instruction." [47] A river of ink has been poured out in an attempt to reconstruct the process by which the early liturgical drama escaped from the rituals of the church and got, eventually, into the marketplace in the form of the cycles. The fact is that very little knowledge has been forthcoming, very few documents have survived to tell the story, and conjecture has run riot with a very small garland of facts.[48]

On the other hand, it is well to keep clearly in mind the matters that are certain about this drama. Above all, the simplest, most evident, and perhaps most basic characteristic of the scriptural cycles is the "desire to convey edifying instruction" that lies behind and informs the matter and manner of even the latest cycles. Nothing in the *Ordinalia* suggests that the drama lacks any of this motivating spirit; in fact, the instructional impulse stands out as the obtrusive and salient feature of the work, even though the ties to the liturgy and doctrine are not so evident to the modern reader as to the medieval spectator. Literary criticism has seldom wavered far from Sidney's Horatian dictum that the aims of a poet are "to teach and to delight," and even a modern writer can hold that "drama shows us what ought to be. It is on the move toward perfection of the individual and the social order." [49] Some such awareness probably lies behind one scholar's opinion that "the Cornish playwright's skillful use of doctrine enabled him to create a play that would be moving even for a secular modern audience." [50] Yet the serious student must be wary of using his own aesthetic responses to evaluate this drama. The desire to make medieval plays dramatically effective in contemporary terms can easily lead to the distorting and misunderstanding of a literature that is securely anchored in the distant past, particularly since its anchorage is a symbolic and ideological tradition that has been either discarded or severely changed.

The business at hand is better served by recognizing that the aims of the drama, or at least of this particular drama, were, to begin with, rather narrowly didactic and instructional. The *Ordinalia* does not establish its dramatic claims in any of the ways by which the modern spectator is prepared to judge the theater. Characterization is crude at best, and nearly all the characters are rigid stereotypes. The formal speech and decorous inactivity of God the Father preserves the metallic dignity of a plane figure exalted; the central role of Jesus is empty of what is today called human interest, full howsoever it may be of doctrinal weight; even the demons talk in a relatively lusterless fashion. Indeed, the figures in the *Ordinalia* are clothes upon old sticks—one almost adds, "to scare a bird." The rather rare efforts at comic byplay do not exhibit the supple wit that has been admired elsewhere in the medieval cycles, as for example and most notably in the *Second Shepherds' Play* of the Towneley cycle. The normal rhythms and variegation of dialogue are in the main quite buried in a form that requires the speakers to converse by stanzas rather than by lines or sentences. These statements are all generalizations for which exceptions can, indeed, be found,[51] but they may be broadly applied with fairness to the *Ordinalia* as a whole. The point is simply that the sources of strength or dramatic vigor in this drama are not where the modern critic is wont to look. It is therefore fitting to consider more closely the purposes which may have been responsible for the genesis and development of the *Ordinalia*.

The thirteenth and fourteenth centuries, the period to which the *Ordinalia* belongs, are notable, among other things, for producing in Europe a considerable body of works devoted to religious instruction. Saints' lives, collections of homilies, handbooks and manuals that illustrated and clarified doctrinal, sacramental, and liturgical matters: numerous such works found their way at this time into the vernacular languages. Thus they testify to the resurgent concern in the church for transmitting the ancient wisdom. The laity no less than the clergy were the beneficiaries, or were at any rate the focus, of this energetic effort. To a considerable extent the vernacular drama may be seen as part of the same impulse that produced these instructional handbooks. The similarity has not been overlooked by scholars, and there have been attempts to trace the drama directly to such sources.[52]

This intensification of religious instruction in the vernacular languages suggests the nature of forces that were at work within the church, and a pre-eminent circumstance at that time was the rising importance of the new religious orders, among which the Dominicans and Franciscans were most notable. After the early thirteenth century the monasteries themselves declined in importance,[53] but the coming of the friars worked a demonstrable change on the life of Britain, and, as one scholar puts it, "for nearly two hundred years the theological life of England . . . was directed and dominated by the friars," [54] as well through their control over learning at the universities as through the influence of the itinerant mendicants and preachers.

The new orders certainly carried with them an impulse toward broadening learning, and as mendicancy rose in significance the influence of these teachers and preachers spread. Another symptom of this change was the effect of the decrees of the Fourth Lateran Council. The Council, which had met in 1215, had aimed most of its seventy synodal canons at the reformation of the clergy, and not the least of the reforming concerns was the evidently widespread scandal of clerical illiteracy.[55] A principal effect of the subsequent reform was a self-conscious program for the dissemination of religious knowledge among the unlearned, both clerical and lay. The instructional materials that began to appear in the thirteenth century probably owe their abundance and their fervor to this conciliar effort at ecclesiastical reform.[56]

Then, too, not least of the achievements of the thirteenth century is the triumph of Scholasticism, most remarkably in the person of St. Thomas Aquinas (1225–1274). Indeed, a useful symbol for the importance of the new spiritual forces that sought more widely to disseminate the religious wealth of the church is the promulgation in the late thirteenth century of the Feast of Corpus Christi. The feast appears to be a kind of liturgical catechesis, aimed at drawing the attention as well as the devotion of the faithful to the eucharistic sacrifice. The religious drama eventually became associated with this feast, and the great Dominican Doctor himself wrote the famous and, in its way, instructional hymn *Pange, lingua,* which is part of the commemorative office for the festival.

Into this broad perspective Cornwall must be placed tenderly, but nonetheless definitely. The foundation at Glasney of the collegiate Church of the Blessed Virgin Mary and St. Thomas-of-Canterbury by the Bishop of Exeter, Walter Bronescombe, in about 1265, drew together a band of secular canons. Since it is generally conceded that the college of canons at Glasney is the most likely place from which the *Ordinalia* might have issued, the event may be seen as a first cause of the drama. The proximate cause is more conjectural. The *Ordinalia* was probably written and produced in order to take advantage of an opportunity to convey religious instruction. It may be that in the long run its survival was due less to any widespread fondness for instruction than to the inherent appeal of its dramatic spectacle and to the genial wish, on the part of the festival crowds, to be entertained. Few, if any, concessions to the popular theatrical appetite are apparent in the work, however, and the *Ordinalia* comes down to us with its didactic force very much intact.

However delightful the *Ordinalia* may have proved to the lay audiences, no evidence exists to suggest that it ever came principally under civic auspices. It is as likely that the drama was to the end in the hands of the clergy as that it came under the control of any other group. In fact, the student may reasonably speculate that the canons themselves perhaps acted in the drama, at least for some time. Chambers, for example, cites a notice of a performance at Cividale, taken from Giuliano da Cividale's *Cronaca Friulana,* in 1303: "Anno MCCCIII facta fuit *per Clerum, sive per Capitulum civitatense,* Repraesentatio: sive factae fuerunt Repraesentationes infra scriptae: In primis, de Creatione primorum parentum; deinde de Annunciatione Beatae Virginis, de Partu et aliis multis, et de Passione et Resurrectione, Ascensione et Adventu Spiritus Sancti, et de Antichristo et aliis, et demum de Adventu Christi ad iudicium. Et predicta facta fuerunt solemniter in curia domini Patriarchae in festo Pentecostes cum aliis duobus diebus sequentibus." (In the year 1303 by the clergy, or rather by the diocesan chapter, a performance was presented, or rather performances were presented, dealing with the following subjects: on the first day, the Creation of our first parents; then the Annunciation to the Blessed Virgin, the Nativity and many other things, and the Passion and Resurrection, the Ascension and the Coming of the Holy Spirit, and the Antichrist and so forth; and finally the coming of Christ in Judgment. And these performances were solemnly presented as described in the court of the Lord Archbishop on the feast of Pentecost and on the two following days.) [57]

As I have pointed out, no evidence is available to establish that the *Ordinalia* was even presented, much less to indicate the nature of its presentation. This note simply records the performance, in Cividale during the feast of Pentecost in 1303, of a cycle of plays by the clergy or the diocesan chapter. The dialogue was presumably rehearsed in Latin; nonetheless, it is significant that a cycle, already well if not fully developed, was at that date regarded highly enough by the church to be presented by the clergy, with ecclesiastical patronage, and, what is more, on an occasion of more than seasonal importance. Although a good deal of effort has gone into establishing the early and general secularization of the drama, this particular evidence urges at least some reluctance to assume that secular patronage everywhere abounded. It is well to be aware of what in the drama retains its religious character and of what sort of religious character it is descriptive.

While secularization of the drama, as a tendency that may be seen generally to have developed in the Middle Ages, has been largely accepted and frequently dealt with, it has often been overemphasized, and too little attention has been paid to the religious forces that are preponderantly at work even in the drama at its most secular. The aim of the present study is to explore the Cornish *Ordinalia* less for the dramatic qualities than for the religious ideas that it contains; in effect, to set aside the question of its dramatic appeal in order to consider the moral, theological, and doctrinal ideas with which it deals and by which it developed in the church.

The *Ordinalia* lends itself particularly well to such a study, partly because it manifests so few of the qualities, apart from the use of the vernacular, that an audience bent more on entertainment than on instruction would have demanded; partly because its Celtic affinities, its provenience, and the circumstances of its presumable presentation indicate that it remained ecclesiastically more continent than most of its English analogues; partly because it has been—quite unjustly—so little studied in the past. This inquiry leads not to the deep wells of medieval thought but to the broad streams where ideas and beliefs met and took on a popular shape and power. The drama, after all, aimed at the popular, as distinct from the ruminative, mind. It does not belong to the history of medieval philosophy, but it is at least a significant part of medieval thought. The *Ordinalia* is rich in the ore that yields such metal. It is frankly and unapologetically didactic in conception as well as execution. The present study, therefore, seeks to examine it as didactics: to point out, that is, what appear to be the basic doctrinal lessons that it seeks to inculcate, and to notice in what ways and by recourse to what ideological idioms the drama goes about its task of instruction in the established religious currency of its day.

2. *The* Ordinalia *and the Bible:*
Interpreting the Old Testament

My *God*, my *God*, Thou art a *direct God*, may I not say, a *literall God*, a *God* that wouldest bee understood *literally*, and according to the *plaine sense* of all that thou saiest? But thou art also (*Lord* I intend it to thy *glory*, and let no *prophane misinterpreter* abuse it to thy *diminution*) thou art a *figurative*, a *metaphoricall God too*: a *God* in whose words there is such a height of *figures*, such *voyages*, such *peregrinations* to fetch remote and precious *metaphors*, such *extentions*, such *spreadings*, such *Curtaines* of *Allegories*, such *third Heavens* of *Hyperboles*, so *harmonious eloquutions*, so *retired* and so *reserved expressions*, so *commanding perswasions*, so *perswading commandements*, such *sinewes* even in thy *milke*, and such things in thy *words*, as all *prophane Authors*, seeme of the seed of the Serpent, that *creepes*, thou art the *Dove*, that flies.[1]

BEHIND Donne's rhapsodic prose lies a long tradition in Christian exegetical theology, and his wary discrimination might profitably stand as an example to modern students of that tradition. The God who is both "literall" and "figurative" defines an approach not only to scriptural revelation and its exposition but also to the fundamental assumptions of Christian theology. This paradoxical attitude toward God characterizes most Christian apologetic literature. What lies behind the paradox is a conviction that while God has taken part in history, he is nonetheless above time and change and all historical qualifications. This belief is essential for an under-

standing of orthodox christology. To Jesus himself the fourth evangelist attributes the affirmation "Before Abraham was, I am" (John
8:58); Paul is careful to insist on a pre-existent Christ; and the
author of the letter to the Hebrews confronts the matter at the
beginning of his exposition: "In many and various ways God spoke
of old to our fathers by the prophets; but in these last days he has
spoken to us by a Son, whom he appointed the heir of all things,
through whom also he created the world" (1:1-2).

The first work of the Christian apologist, then, has ever been
to explain or to justify this paradox, at the heart of which is a
view of history. The Bible embodies the sequence of events—the
history—that shapes and informs the interpretive method. What
one scholar has written apropos of Rabanus Maurus' attitude
toward the Bible may in a large sense be applied to every thinker
in the mainstream of Christian orthodoxy: "the Bible was divided
into two essentially different halves, one the audible and visible
material word which told a story, the other the transcendent moral
or allegorical sense telling of spiritual truths." [2]

The medieval dramatist was, like Donne, heir to this tradition.
Donne, however, invokes the tradition verbally and explicitly, to
justify his own imaginative procedures. The dramatist relied on
implication; and, in fact, the paradox was part of his matter itself.
Since the *Ordinalia,* like the other cycles, deals with the main
mystery of the Christian religion by dramatizing the "history" on
which that mystery depends, the dramatist was perforce concerned
with the theological and interpretive materials that were available
to him. Neither the choice of incidents nor the theological import
of his dramatization rested entirely with the dramatist himself. The
theological tradition in which the medieval religious play properly
belongs rather required of the dramatist the ability to evince a
more or less self-explanatory scriptural exegesis. He had to balance
the dramatic claims of his work against the theological meaning
with which, for the sake of instruction, he wished to freight it.

The drama did not, to be sure, labor alone amongst the arts

under this theological strain. Painting and sculpture, for example, were often valued more highly as means of instruction than as vehicles for creative expression or aesthetic experience.[3] The Venerable Bede recalls that upon Benedict Biscop's return to the Abbey of Wearmouth and Jarrow from his fourth visit to Rome in 684, he brought with him, to adorn the walls of the recently built abbey church, a number of decorative images—*picturas imaginum sanctarum*—that were intended for the edification of the unlettered worshipers.[4] The catechistic impulse, thus already manifest in the eighth century, was everywhere apparent by the fourteenth.

The instruction that the laity may be presumed to have required was no doubt basic, and it is necessary to ascertain what that basic instruction involved. To do so requires, in one scholar's felicitous phrase, a venture on to the "troubled sea of Biblical exegesis," [5] and begins in the attempt to discern the fundamental ideas that are involved in the effort to explain Scripture. In recent years this general subject has received a great deal of study, and the results have been confusing as well as conflicting, while the discussion has been at times acrimonious.[6] Although the scholarly caldron thus still seethes, the matter is important, and to make sense of the issues as well as the ideas in which the issues are embedded requires some understanding of the bases of medieval exegesis and an awareness of how, as well as the more arguable matter of into what, it evolved.

Along with the fundamental theological paradox of God as both determining and participating in the course of history, St. Paul makes a number of important distinctions. He contrasts the "law" and the "spirit"; he speaks of a "new creation" as implicitly distinct from what was; he compares the "wisdom of men" and the "folly of God." While the distinctions are not all of the same order, their presence indicates a sense of separation—or at least an inclination toward a double vision—that is deeply woven into Pauline thought, and is furthermore and consequently a significant characteristic of Christian exegesis.[7] This point has not always been properly emphasized in modern speculation about the form or content or purpose of exegesis.

In the first place, the cliché that a "fourfold sense" of scriptural interpretation was widely practiced by early and medieval exegetes is not in itself properly descriptive or explanatory of the method and aims of this traditional kind of biblical commentary. According to the "fourfold sense," the Bible contains various levels of meaning. It is always and foremost a historical record, and may so be read; it bears also a weight of allegory; it has a moral significance; it is finally anagogical, and points to eternity. An example customarily cited is William Durandus' explanation of the significance of the city Jerusalem.[8] Such a scheme is clearly a model and not a rigid framework. To be sure, the manifest absurdity of any attempt to apply this fourfold sense systematically to the Bible did not always deter medieval systematizers, nor does it always occur to modern simplifiers. Of more immediate concern to the student of the drama, however, are the reasons for, as well as the utility and significance of, such an exegetical model.

Theologically, as I have suggested, this interpretive procedure functions as a means of dealing with the Christian view of history. It organizes itself around the historical personage of Jesus Christ, who represents the fulfillment of God's purposes. The consequent division or bifurcation of time is a historical attitude of which the manifold exegetical approach is a defining theological characteristic. The Bible, then, relates a sequence of events that begins at creation and looks to terminate at the end of time. The fourfold sense of exegesis accepts this linear process, but attempts to join with it a teleological view of Christ as the center and focus by which any single event in the sequence can be measured and evaluated. Thus, as Lubac persuasively argues, the fourfold sense of exegesis is fundamentally a dichotomy, a division predicated on an open and apparent meaning over against which is set an inner and mystical meaning. He cites Nicholas de Lyra (ca. 1270–1340) to support this argument that the scheme is basically a bifurcation: "Scriptura exterior est sensus litteralis, qui est patentior, quia per voces immediate significatur; Scriptura vero interior, est sensus mysticus, vel spiritualis, qui est latentior, quia per res significatas vocibus designatur." (The external part of the Holy Scriptures is the literal meaning, which is more accessible because it is made known directly through what is said; but the internal part is the mystical, or spiritual meaning, which is more hidden because it is designated through the things made known by what is said.) [9] This second and inner, or mystical, signification has, in turn, usually broken into three parts—so that allegory, tropology, and anagogy are various avenues leading to the mystical meaning, as the several requirements of doctrine demand.

If Christ is the center of history, then the primary event by which he merits that centrality is the Redemption, an act that serves at once as the motivation for his exegetical method and as the ground theme of the medieval drama.[10] Erich Auerbach says simply that in Christian thought, "History is the drama of Redemption." [11] The Redemption is a theological idea embedded in a historical action—the death and resurrection of Christ. The action itself divides history, establishes the central paradox with which I have dealt briefly and generally above, and traditionally provides the fundamental premise of Christian thought.

Consequently, exegesis is preoccupied with this event. The New Testament no less than the liturgy, doctrine, and theology of the Church, revolves about the event and its implications. Biblically, the work of Redemption separates the Old Law from the New, and therefore the hidden from the revealed, the expectation from the fulfillment, the creation of the world from the "new creation" of which Paul speaks. By extension, this exegetical view supposes "that there is an imperfect order which prepares for and prefigures an order of perfection." [12] With this basic attitude firmly established, the exegete could make use of the tools most conveniently at hand to elucidate the mystical significance of the work with which he dealt. Thus, Hugh of St. Victor (ca. 1096–1141)

could write that "it is necessary . . . so to handle the Sacred
Scripture that we do not try to find history everywhere, nor allegory
everywhere, nor tropology everywhere, but rather that we assign
individual things fittingly in their own places, as reason demands." [13]
It will be noted that Hugh uses a different interpretive scheme
than the customary fourfold method. This threefold approach apparently goes back at least to Origen (ca. 185–ca. 254), where it
is generally analogous, at any rate in intent, as Lubac points out,
to the tripartite division of man into body, soul, and spirit, and to
"the three successive reigns of the law, of grace, and, beyond that,
of the spirit." [14] The threefold and fourfold schemes are not so very
different in practice, however, and Hugh of St. Victor seems generally more concerned with the distinction between literal and
mystical meanings than with mounting a consistently three-pronged
attack. As Bloomfield has pointed out, "except for typology . . .
at no time did any biblical exegete repudiate the importance and
often the primacy of the biblical letter." [15]

If the Redemption is at once part of a series of related events
and at the same time, in the person of the Redeemer, a kind of
spiritual first cause upon which all events depend, then it embodies
at its center a teleology: in effect, this one event is both ultimate
and seminal. It is the fulfillment of all prior history and the standard by which all subsequent history can be measured. The manifold exegetical scheme incorporates this teleology, particularly at
its mystical levels, for the various means of interpreting the Bible
are concerned with this central event.

Nor is it surprising that the medieval drama should itself be
exegetical. The relationship between traditional exegesis and the
drama is important because the cycles concern themselves fundamentally with biblical episodes and are, in effect, a means of relat-
ing and explaining those episodes theologically as well as dramatically.[16] That the author of the Cornish *Ordinalia* is aware not only
of the immediate demands of biblical interpretation but also of its
implications and ultimate concerns is evident from the beginning,

when Deus Pater emerges to introduce himself and to set in motion
the drama:

> En tas a nef y'm gylwyr
>   formyer pup tra a vyt gvrys
> Onan ha try on yn gvyr
>   en tas ha'n map ha'n spyrys
> ha hethyv me a thesyr
>   dre ov grath dalleth an beys.

(The father of heaven I am called, the creator of all things that
are made. One and three we are in truth, the father, and the son,
and the spirit; and this day I desire by my grace to begin the world:
OM 1–6.)

These lines at once affirm the theological center or preoccupation of the drama and manifest the fundamental paradox in the
historical scheme. The drama simply opens with the creation, itself a historical process. By invoking the trinitarian formula, however, Deus Pater introduces the mystical dimensions of history. The
allusion to the Trinity might strike a spectator as merely a casual
creedal or liturgical echo, and to the modern ear it may sound dramatically anachronistic; nonetheless, theologically and exegetically,
mystical deep is calling unto mystical deep. Within the Old Testament record of creation ("In the beginning God created the heavens
and the earth") now reverberates the New Testament christology
("In the beginning was the Word, and the Word was with God").

Indeed, this same view of history informs the drama's elaborate use of episodes drawn from the Old Testament. With Jesus and
his work of redemption as the focus of the drama, all that intervenes between the creation and his first appearance both dramatically and theologically relies on a steady rise in expectancy toward
that functional fulfillment. The theological method employed to
sustain such a relationship is ably summed up in the use to which
St. Gregory puts a metaphor taken from the prophet Ezekiel:
"Rota intra rotam est Testamentum Novum . . . intra Testamentum Vetus, quia quod designavit Testamentum Vetus, hoc

Testamentum Novum exhibuit" (A wheel within a wheel is the New Testament . . . within the Old, for what the Old Testament pointed to, the New showed forth).[17]

This relationship between the Old and New Testaments is used liberally and abundantly by the church fathers and by their successors.[18] Seldom, however, is the full implication of the exegetical attitude so apparent as it is here. The method—itself apparent in Gregory's remark—by which this relationship is reconstructed centers in typological exegesis. At the outset, it is well to turn to St. Augustine for a fundamental explanation of the method:

Ante omnia tamen, fratres, hoc in nomine Domini et admonemus, quantum possumus, et praecipimus, ut quando auditis exponi sacramentum Scripturae narrantis quae gesta sunt, prius illud quod lectum est credatis sic gestum, quomodo lectum est; ne subtracto fundamento rei gestae, quasi in aere quaeratis aedificare. Abraham pater noster homo erat illis temporibus fidelis, credens Deo, justificatus ex fide, sicut Scriptura dicit, et vetus et nova . . . Quidquid Scriptura dicit de Abraham, et factum est, et prophetia est: sicut Apostolus quodam loco dicit, *Scriptum est enim quod Abraham duos filios habuit; unum de ancilla, et alterum de libera: quae sunt in allegoria. Haec ergo sunt duo Testamenta.* [Galatians 4:22, 24.]

(Nevertheless, brothers, before all things, in the name of the Lord we both warn you and enjoin upon you, so far as we are able, that when you hear an exposition of the mystery of a text of Holy Scripture that tells what things were done, first believe that which is read literally, as having happened in the manner in which it is reported, lest by depriving the event of its historical foundation you act as if you would build in air. Abraham our father was a faithful man in those times, trusting in God and justified by faith, according to the Scriptures, both the old and the new . . . Whatever the Scriptures say about Abraham is both actuality and prophecy: as the Apostle says somewhere, 'For it is written, that Abraham had two sons, the one by a bondmaid, the other by a freewoman . . . Which things are an allegory: for these are the two covenants.') [19] This insistence on the literal as well as the prophetic significance of the Bible, the *sacramentum Scripturae,* is an essential admonition and is fundamental to an understanding of the relationship between the Old and New Testaments assumed in most early exegesis. Typology does not contravene this relationship; it is rather a formulaic shorthand that implicitly affirms the relationship along with the exegetical view of history.

First of all, then, Abraham is a historical personage. Secondly, he is a prophetic figure, a type. The explanation by St. Basil (ca. 330–379) may be taken as definitive: "the type is a manifestation (*delosis*) of things to come through an imitation (*mimesis*) allowing us to see in advance the things of the future in such wise that they can be understood." [20] On the one hand, events are precisely what they seem to be: they relate sequentially, they are descriptive of physical reality, they limit and define human experience. On the other hand, they are more or less different from what they seem to be: they are prophetic and prefigure other events, they are types of spiritual reality, they enlarge and generalize human experience. Events thus treated as symbols become, mystically rather more than historically, part of the "economy of salvation." [21]

Typology, then, is an instrument of scriptural interpretation that is faithful to both aspects of the fourfold scheme—the literal, that is, as well as the mystical meaning of what it explains.[22] The unity is rather more doctrinal and implicit than everywhere apparent, and typology lends itself easily to a distortion of this central relationship,[23] but, in the main, biblical interpretation was faithful to this exegetical paradox, and it may safely be taken as a guiding principle.

It is hard to tell how much of the typological or figurative significance of the Old Testament episodes may be presumed to have been intended by the dramatist or to have been recognized by the average layman as a spectator at the drama. The dramatist, of course, does not openly remark that Abel's murder prefigures

Christ's death on the cross, or that Isaac's deliverance from sacrifice intentionally anticipates the resurrection. Nonetheless, he does indeed supply some verbal and visual indications that he sees typological significance in the events that he draws from the Old Testament. Moses' dying prayer, for example, implicitly recalls that he is a type of Christ:

> arluth dev ker klew ov lef
> ha gor vy the lowene
> ha'm spyrys thy'so ressef
> *in manus tuuas domine.*

(Dear Lord God, hear my voice, and bring me to bliss; and receive my spirit to thee, *in manus tuas Domine: OM* 1895–1898).

The Latin tag is, of course, an allusion to the last words attributed by the evangelist Luke to Christ at his death (Luke 23:46), which may, in turn, be a quotation of Psalms 31:5. In the biblical account of Moses' death there is no such last speech, and later in the Cornish passion Jesus himself utters these words in the vernacular:

> A tas yntre the thule
> my a gemmyn ow spyrys.

(O father, between thy hands I commit my spirit: *PC* 2985–2986.) The deliberate quotation of an easily recognized Latin phrase draws attention forcibly to the relationship between Moses and Christ; the macaronic interpolation would have been suggestive of the liturgy as well; and it is fitting that Moses, who is the central personage under the law, should anticipate the act of grace by which the law was to be fulfilled and superseded. Moses' act as well as his speech is therefore typological: the prophet's death points toward Jesus' death.[24] Dramatically, too, this allusion appropriately prepares for the climax of the drama in the crucifixion and resurrection.

While the dramatist was clearly aware of the paramount exegetical importance of typology and wrote accordingly, the drama

seldom suggests typological correspondences so overtly as in the
death of Moses, and the spectator may have been far less assured
of the typological significance of what he saw than we may wish
everywhere to suppose. Henry Jenner some time ago recognized
the value of a knowledge of typology in studying the drama, but he
was perhaps too enthusiastic when he observed that "to the mediaeval Christian the whole value of the Old Testament was in its
being made up of recognised types of the New, and slight allusions
. . . would be well understood." [25] And it is disputable that, in
the religious drama, "rare were the hearers or spectators who felt
the need to meditate on the cogency of the more or less factitious
correspondences that slothful minds preferred to admit without
question." [26]

Although, to be sure, the medieval Christian may have been
well aware of the significance of types and figures through the liturgy, sermons, and plastic arts in his churches, typology is nonetheless based on correspondences that are indeed "more or less
factitious" and often liable to confusion. If, on the one hand, there
was a remarkable visual example to be seen in the typological cycle
fashioned by Nicholas of Verdun (ca. 1180) on the altar at the
abbey of Klosterneuburg,[27] on the other hand the popular story of
David and Bathsheba was in some quarters so tormented that the
lovers could prefigure Christ and the Church while the wronged
husband Uriah represented the Jewish people or the glory of God
usurped by the devil.[28] The Cornish dramatist, though he uses the
incident, does not, I hasten to note, fall prey to this curious Davidic
typology, for the King is made properly aware of the divine wrath
through the parable of the "poor man's lamb" (2 Samuel 12:1-6)
—the angel Gabriel rather than the prophet Nathan is the dramatist's messenger—and he is left in sackcloth and ashes singing a
penitential hymn. Nonetheless, the very artificial character of typology, evident in this example, makes liable to suspicion any
nascent certitude about the layman's ease in perceiving types.

The history of the development of typological exegesis is

itself a study in frequent confusion, false starts, excessive enthusiasms, and abundant perplexities.[29] It is safe to say, however, that by the twelfth century, the typological relationships were generally established, and were part of the fundamental equipment of all the commentators. An example of the type's slow growth from uncertain and tentative association to confident correspondence can be traced in Puech's study of Psalms 51[50]:12-14, in which verses the three mentions of "spirit" came to be regarded as a Davidic prefiguration of the Trinity: although some types go back to St. Paul, and typology itself in early patristic literature grew haphazardly and by accretion, in this case the germ of the idea is traced to Origen.[30] This method plainly permits abuse when at the mercy of a stimulated imagination, and many voices have been raised in uneasy protest. Hugh of St. Victor reminded commentators who increasingly indulged their allegorical tendencies in exegesis about the primacy of *historia* in the Scriptures; Roger Bacon (ca. 1214–1292) chafed against the phantasmic excesses of typology in his own time; and a contemporary scholar has felt compelled to remember that Christ himself "affirms that all which concerns him in the Scriptures will come true, not that the entire Old Testament has reference directly to himself." [31]

The dramatist himself is remarkably faithful to the Old Testament history and, in the case of the wood of the cross, to traditional legend. Adam is first of all Adam, and only by grace of interpretive tradition a type of Christ. Finally, it is well to remember the imperfect character of the type: "Each of the types of Christ in the Old Testament brings out some aspect of the redemption," [32] and none fully encompasses the mystery of its antitype.

The *Ordinalia* begins with the creation, and throughout this first episode nothing is more evident than the playwright's insistence on the trinitarian identity of God. Deus Pater himself alludes to the three persons three times in his opening proclamation (*OM* 3–4, 12–13, 57–58). Upon his creation, Adam immediately addresses his creator as a trinity:

A das map ha spyrys sans,
gorthyans the'th corf wek pup prys

(O father, son, and holy spirit, worship to thy sweet body always: *OM* 85–86); and when Eve is fashioned of Adam's rib, she voices her gratitude and proclaims an orthodox creed: "vn dev os ha persons try" (Thou art one God, and three persons: *OM* 110). What seems historically anachronistic in these asseverations is, as I have noted, mystically, and therefore typologically, entirely acceptable. Indeed, not even Adam's allusion to "thy sweet body" (*the'th corf wek*) is unintentional, for the phrase suggests the allegiance due the *corpus christi,* and its association with the essential mystery in the sacrifice of the Mass. Besides, God created man *ad imaginem, et similitudinem suam,* and the trinitarian nature of God is reflected in the threefold nature of man as body, soul, and spirit.

While nothing in this representation of creation is either unorthodox or sheer embroidery, the insistence on the Trinity is a doctrinal or theological point that is not essential to a literal understanding of the biblical story of the creation. The intrusion certainly indicates that the exegetical mind is at work in the drama, for the doctrine is used fundamentally as an interpretive device.

Doctrinally, the creation anticipates the redemption, which in the person of Christ symbolizes a "new creation," in the language of St. Paul. Therefore the creation has, in its own right but more especially as a type, a sacramental quality: [33] "For in Christ Jesus neither circumcision availeth any thing, nor uncircumcision, but a new creature" (Galatians 6:15). The dramatist, like the theologians in whose path he follows, labors "to make all men see what is the plan of the mystery hidden for ages in God—*dispensatio sacramenti absconditi a saeculis in Deo*—who created all things" (Ephesians 3:9), and the beginning of the *dispensatio sacramenti absconditi* is the creation.

After the creation the *Ordinalia* takes up the temptation and the fall. A proper grasp of this episode involves not so much a theological comprehension of a Miltonic issue between free will and

right knowledge as a typological appreciation for the *felix culpa*
and the Pauline relationship between Adam and Christ. The
serpent clumsily beguiles Eve, who seduces Adam by forcing him
to choose between his love for her and his obedience to God, but
the climax of the episode yet remains. After God has judged and
condemned each of the recreants in three separate two-stanza
speeches, Adam's plea and God's response dominate the scene:

Adam

A das dev y'th wolowys
grannt the'th whythres my a'd peys
nep peyth a oel a vercy.

Deus Pater

Adam yn dyweth a'n beys
my a wronnt oel mercy they's
ha the eua the wreghty.

(*Adam:* O father, God, in thy light grant to thy workmanship, I
pray thee, some of the oil of mercy. *God the Father:* Adam, in the
end of the world I will grant the oil of mercy to thee, and to Eve thy
wife: *OM* 325–330.)

This non-biblical pledge is, to be sure, part of the legendary
material on which the Cornish dramatist draws; but it is also an
exegetical device that links the fall with a much later episode, the
Harrowing of Hell, when, after Christ has delivered Adam and
Eve and their patriarchal descendants from the dominion of
Satan, the Spirit of Christ holds a colloquy with Adam. In the
course of that dialogue Adam echoes the terms of this promise
when he addresses Christ: "merci pysaf" (I pray mercy: *RD* 148);
when he affirms to Enoch in heaven,

ow arluth cryst dr'y vercy
a wruk ow dysprenne vy
mes a yfarn yn teffry

(My Lord Christ, by his mercy, did indeed redeem me out of hell:
RD 215–217); and when his latter-day kinsman, the thief Dismas,
to whom a place in paradise was promised at the crucifixion, in-

forms him that "cryst yw arluth a vercy" (Christ is the lord of mercy: *RD* 283). The expectation of mercy and its fulfillment thus joins the Old Law with the New, and the reign of sin with the rule of grace. Though Adam is perhaps the most familiar, he is a most peculiar, type of Christ,[34] for his sin does not properly prefigure the redemption, but makes it possible. Therefore the fall is a *felix culpa,* and Paul can speak of Adam as *forma futuri* (typos mellontos): "yet death reigned from Adam to Moses, even over those whose sins were not like the transgression of Adam, who was a type of the one who was to come" (Romans 5:14).[35] Thus in medieval paintings of the crucifixion, Adam's skull generally appears at the foot of the cross. This commonly recognized typology did not fail to delight John Donne:

> We think that Paradise and Calvary,
>   Christ's cross and Adam's tree, stood in one place;
> Look Lord, and find both Adams met in me.[36]

The unlettered spectator may therefore be presumed without impropriety to have recognized in this brief exchange at least something of the exegetical and dramatic relationship between what he was seeing and what he expected subsequently to see—the life of Christ which was to follow. On the other hand, the dramatist has not made the whole business self-evident. The allusion is unobtrusive enough, and Adam's plea for mitigation is, under the circumstances, sufficiently plausible, so that the episode remains theologically subtle though effective, while it dissipates none of its dramatic power in abstrusely symbolic signification.

In the brief subsequent scene, again not biblical, Adam discovers that he is unable to till the ground since, when he attempts to dig, the earth cries out and refuses to be violated. This terrene recalcitrance may follow from God's speech, *maledicta terra in opere tuo* (Genesis 3:17; cf. *OM* 271–272); at any rate, the consequent interchange between Adam and God the Father, in which Adam wheedles permission first to cut a spade's length (*OM* 380), then three lengths (*OM* 392), and finally as much as he wishes

(*OM* 403–404), does not, so far as I am aware, have its counterpart in medieval drama, nor have I found it treated thus elsewhere. It may have as its intention a reminder that sullied Adam is attempting to defile the unsullied earth from which he was formed, since an old tradition, exemplified in Irenaeus and in subsequent writers, describes the earth as Adam's "virgin mother," an obvious allusion to the virgin birth of Christ.[37]

Even if this be the ideological justification for the scene, it is important to recognize first that this brief episode places another problem, generally unnoticed, in the way of the occasional facile assumption that the Cornish plays are simply derivative; and secondly that it has its dramatic justification as well. The semisolemn, semicomic exchange provides a relatively smooth transition for Adam from his exalted state in paradise to the fallen state in which he and his descendants thenceforth must dwell. Man's fall from grace is itself a powerful theme, and the unmitigated harshness with which he is banished from paradise can easily awaken pathos. The Cornish dramatist hastens to avoid that danger, and in the exchange between Adam and his creator, the father of men haggles and whines over his heritance in the decidedly unpathetic language of the marketplace. Here, as elsewhere, the author indulges in his favorite form of mercantile comic byplay, the dispute over proper measurement: later, the beam of the temple is cut either too short or too long (*OM* 2520f), and the nail holes in the cross are bored too far apart (*PC* 2754f).

The murder of Abel, which follows, is another richly typological episode. The themes of sacrifice, murder, and treachery obviously enough connect this event with the betrayal and death of Christ. Once again, however, the dramatist eschews too blatant a comparison. And again, his slight divergence from the biblical account involves principally the theological idea of mercy. In Genesis 4:3–7 God asserts his preference for Abel's sacrifice by admonishing Cain; in the *Ordinalia* Deus Pater ignores Cain and assures Abel that

ef a'n gefyth yn dyweth
an ioy na thyfyk nefre
yn ov gulas ha cosoleth.

(He [Abel] shall in the end find unfailing joy ever in my land, and
rest: *OM* 516–518.) Then after he has slain Abel, Cain, like
Judas later, falls into the heresy of believing his sin to be greater
than the mercy of God (*OM* 591–592). These embellishments en-
rich the scene with a sense of the expectation and reverberation
upon which figurative exegesis rests. The whole attitude gains dramatic depth when the devils take Abel away to hell, certain that he
is their prisoner forever; their self-confidence juxtaposed with
God's assurance of "unfailing joy" establishes the tension that anticipates the redemption.[38]

Two minor details in this episode indicate the dramatist's
awareness of typological correspondence, although neither can be
assumed to have been obvious to the auditors. In the *Ordinalia*
Deus Pater specifically requests that the sacrifice be made on Mount
Tabor (*OM* 429). The biblical account makes no mention of this
mountain. It recurs in the *Ordinalia* as the place where Moses
plants the three rods and dies.[39] In fact, Moses died, according to
the Bible, on Mount Nebo, at the "top of Pisgah" (Deuteronomy
34:1f). The dramatist, however, looks here to a later tradition,
according to which Mount Tabor was regarded as the site of the
transfiguration, the occasion when Moses appeared with Elias to
glorify Jesus in the presence of his disciples. The localization of the
event on Mount Tabor was suggested at least as early as Cyril of
Jerusalem (ca. 315–386).[40] Mount Tabor seems to function gen-
erically in the *Ordinalia* as a holy mountain.

Then, too, the allusion to the blood of Abel "ov kelwel a'n
dor" (calling from the ground: *OM* 578–579), although it is found
in Genesis 4:10 ("vox sanguinis fratris tui clamat ad me de terra"
—the voice of thy brother's blood crieth unto me from the ground),
was used typologically by the writer of the epistle to the Hebrews:
"et testamenti novi mediatorem Jesum, et sanguinis aspersionem

melius loquentem, quam Abel" ([ye are come] to Jesus the mediator of the new covenant, and to the blood of sprinkling, that speaketh better things than that of Abel—12:24). Thus Abel's blood, which called in judgment, is a sign of Christ's blood, which would at once fulfill and redeem Abel's bloodshed. The conjunction is easily understandable, and the *vox sanguinis fratris* is a powerful and popular metaphor. It occurs, for example, in an Old English maxim: "Wearð fæhþo fyra cynne, siþþan furþum swealg eorðe Abeles blode." (Enmity was with mankind just as soon as the earth swallowed up the blood of Abel.) [41]

The history of Seth then follows in the *Ordinalia*—his birth and visit to Paradise. The journey is not part of biblical account, but belongs to the legendary matter used by the dramatist, and although the incident is important for understanding the drama's view of prechristian history, I shall consider separately the legend of which it is a part. The birth of Seth, on the other hand, following as it does immediately upon Abel's death and the consequent grief of his parents—which leads them to forswear the begetting of further progeny until an angel intervenes to countermand this resolution—belongs to an old and traditional resurrection typology: St. Augustine, in the *City of God,* argues that "in these two men, Abel, signifying 'grief,' and his brother Seth, signifying 'resurrection,' the death of Christ and His life from the dead are prefigured." [42] Although the Cornish dramatist was clearly aware of and used this traditional view of Seth's birth, he does not make the christological comparison particularly evident, and if one may assume that his principal interest in Seth was for Seth's importance in the legend of the cross, he has skillfully and unobtrusively introduced an episode that is faithful to exegetical tradition while it is at the same time dramatically useful in getting Seth onto the stage.

The story of Noah and the flood is the next subject treated in the *Ordinalia*. Again, a natural and popular typological association is available: "No theme occurs more frequently in the Fathers than the symbolism of the ark of Noah as a type of the Church which saves men from divine judgement by means of water." [43] The fertile associations inspired by this juxtaposition are traditionally numerous: "The ark is the Church, Noah is Christ; the dove [is] the Holy Spirit, the olive branch the divine philanthropy;" [44] the raven represents the faithless souls that are departed into outer darkness,[45] and the fatal flood waters prefigure the regenerative water of baptism.[46]

The dramatist, however, not only understates but explicitly avoids this conventional soteriology, for although all the passengers on the ark, "yn onour dev" (in honor of God: *OM* 1169), build an altar on which to offer sacrifices to celebrate their safe return, the incident as a whole is laden with an overwhelming sense of the divine vengeance represented in the flood. Indeed, at the conclusion of the episode Noah and Deus Pater both repeatedly use this word "vengeance" (*dyal*) to characterize the whole affair.[47] Noah insists that man cannot endure a life so threatened by retribution, and even when God promises to eschew vengeance henceforth, Noah reminds him in a display of impertinent outrage that

> ambosow orth tryher bureys
> annethe nynses laha.

(Promises made by the mighty are to them no law: *OM* 1235–1236.) God indulgently rewards this calculated incredulity by arranging for the rainbow to be given as a sign.

The attitude of distrust bred by primitive vengeance is characteristic of Noah throughout the episode. When, for example, God first asks him to make the ark, he replies that since everyone else is to be destroyed, he and his family might as well be included in the general malediction (*OM* 969–72). This emphasis does not particularly interfere with the customary symbolism that compares Noah and the ark to Christ and his church, but it places more importance on the savagery of destruction than on the salvage of righteousness. Noah is still a *typus christi,* but with a difference— and the difference is apparent again in a rare departure from literal fidelity to Scripture. Noah's ark came biblically to rest "upon the

mountains of Ararat" (Genesis 8:4); the honor in the *Ordinalia* is
given to "Mount Calvary" (*OM* 1180), which is identified as the
site of the postdiluvian ritual sacrifice:

> tekke alter yn neppow
> ny alse den aspye
> es del vs genen hep wow
> dres an mount calvarye.

(Without doubt, a man could see no fairer altar in any place than
ours upon Mount Calvary: *OM* 1177–1180.) A more explicit example of typological correspondence could not be asked. The flood
carried Noah to the hill of the crucifixion, where Noah, as later
Christ, erected a peerless altar and sacrificed; indeed sacrificed, if
further comparison were necessary, "yn dewellens pecadow" (in
atonement of sins: *OM* 1173). The concern for "vengeance" only
makes more emphatic the anticipation of the later sacrifice, which
would epitomize the intervention of mercy with which the dramatist has been so concerned.

The sacrifice of Isaac is the classic prefiguration of the resurrection: St. Gregory of Nyssa (ca. 330–ca. 395) observed that "the
whole mystery of faith can be seen in the story of Isaac . . . In the
lamb is revealed the mystery of death and in the only son the life
which will never be cut short by death." [48] The episode is, of course,
in itself inherently dramatic and was eventually to be treated with
exceptional pathos in the later English medieval drama. The
Cornish dramatist, however, exercises an even more remarkable
restraint, as he hurries through this emotional scene in some 130
lines. Exegetically, the scene seems almost parenthetic in the
drama, although it plays a vital part in the traditional interpretation
of the relationship between the Old Law and the New.[49] Since the
redemption is so vital and central in the cycle plays, and particularly
in light of the *Ordinalia*'s conceptual organization about that theme,
it seems odd that the dramatist did not more fully take advantage
of this incident. On the other hand, the story line in the *Origo
Mundi* is moving on the whole in another direction, based on the

legendary history of the cross, which may explain why this scene, though thematically relevant, appears to be a kind of dramatic digression. The dramatist does not discourage a typological application; for example, he adds to the biblical account an almost iconographically visual detail of the wood being bound on Isaac's back as he goes to the sacrifice. The Bible merely remarks that Isaac carried the *lignum holocausti* (the wood of the burnt offering— Genesis 22:6), but often in medieval sculpture Isaac has the wood bound on his back in the shape of a tau cross.

Nonetheless, the intended effect of the incident is difficult to evaluate. The opening lines stress Abraham's fidelity and the importance of the test. Deus Pater says,

> an couath byth ny hassaf
> mar qureth thy'm a'n sacryfys.

(I will never cease from remembering thee, if thou sacrifice him to me: *OM* 1283–1284.) The angel's intervention seems more an act of mercy intended to relieve the suffering of Abraham than part of a plan of deliverance:

> yn pur wyr dev a aswon
> volungeth ol the colon.

(Very truly, God knows all the wish of thy heart: *OM* 1375–1376.) The incident is otherwise so undeviating in its fidelity to the bare outline of the story itself, that any speculation about the dramatist's motives threatens to distort the impulses of the drama.

Moses appears next, to occupy the center of the drama for some time. The burning bush, the deliverance of his people from Egypt and their crossing of the Red Sea, the obtaining of water from a rock in the desert, and incidents in the legendary history of the cross are all included. All the events are compressed, and before attempting to see the exegetical purpose in this set of incidents, it is well to note that each of the scenes manifests first of all a proper dramatic concern; thus, the compressed brevity of the opening exchange between Moses and Deus Pater permits little typological or symbolic expatiation. For example, one tradition saw the staff turned serpent as a prefiguration of the incarnation.[50] The *Ordinalia* presents it rather as a kind of talisman vouchsafed to Moses for his safety (*OM* 1461–1462).

In the crossing of the Red Sea it is perhaps fruitful again to observe where the dramatist departs from the scriptural text. It is not God himself, as in Exodus, but his angel Gabriel who advises Moses how to get across the water; Moses effects the miracle of separating the waters by striking the sea with his talismanic rod (*OM* 1675–1676), whereas in Exodus he merely stretches out his hand over the water (14:21), although he may have held his rod the while (*eleva virgam tuam:* Exodus 14:16); and at the conclusion of the crossing the retinue settles down to build houses, rather than to wander in the wilderness. Still, these divergences are only minor, and if a typological awareness lies behind them, it is probably basically sacramental—for the crossing is a type of baptism, and the principal dramatic focus of the venture is on the felicitous escape from tyranny granted the chosen people and effected through the intermediary, Moses.[51] Both here and in the striking of the rock liturgical awareness is more strongly manifest than elsewhere in the Old Testament drama. While such a concern is at a remove from the christocentricity of most typology in the play, typological exegesis was as useful for sacramental as for biblical history; indeed, to the medieval exegete Paul must have appeared effectively to combine both uses: "Moreover, brethren, I would not that ye should be ignorant, how that all our fathers were under the cloud, and all passed through the sea; and were all baptized unto Moses in the cloud and in the sea; and did all eat the same spiritual meat; and did all drink the same spiritual drink; for they drank of that spiritual Rock that followed them: and that Rock was Christ." (1 Corinthians 10:1–4.)

I have already observed the correspondence between Moses and Christ implicit in the Latin phrase *in manus tuas* used in the *Origo Mundi* by Moses at his death. Even so, the fundamental emphasis is on neither the christological nor the sacramental typology, but rather on the thematic significance of this event for the whole drama. Indeed, this emphasis finally applies to the exegetical character of virtually the entire *Origo Mundi*. Here again, the interposition of mercy weighs most heavily in the drama.

Although Joshua also is traditionally regarded as a type of Christ,[52] in the *Ordinalia* he seems to have no such role. Both Caleb and Joshua, incidentally, are assigned a number of speeches, although they are mentioned by name but once (*OM* 1880). Several of their speeches are probably assigned to them not *in propria persona,* but as a theatrical device for "doubling." Thus, the actors who would play Caleb and Joshua, and to whom are given, respectively, two and one speeches in the plan at the end of the *Origo Mundi,* could conveniently take the parts of First Man and Second Man, who have five and seven speeches, respectively. The parenthetical identification of the First Man and Second Man in the ascriptions directly preceding lines 1611, 1617, and others, is therefore probably a staging suggestion offered by a later hand in the manuscript.

Moses again takes part in the legend of the cross, as does David who follows him, but these incidents will be discussed, with others of their kind, in the chapter following. In addition to his part in this legend, David's affair with Bathsheba and his instigation of the building of the temple are treated in the *Ordinalia*. Indeed, broadly speaking, the remainder of the *Origo Mundi* is given over to the establishment of the temple. Thus, although the affair between David and Bathsheba is dramatically exciting in itself, it is also a prelude to the commission to build the temple, for David is first advised to build the temple as a penitential act (*OM* 2259–2260), and then is refused permission to finish the building on account of his part in the death of Uriah (*OM* 2333–2338). The temple is a foreshadowing of the establishment of the church, and it is only indirectly concerned with christology, although the Cornish dramatist is to seize on it later as the reason for the official hostility toward Jesus: he links the cleansing of the temple (John 2:13f) with the enigmatic asseveration of Jesus, "Solvite templum hoc, et in tribus diebus excitabo illud!" (Destroy this temple, and in three days I will raise it up—John 2:19). Therefore, the concern for the temple in the *Origo Mundi* looks forward to the later role of the church as the mystical body of Christ.

In his treatment of the episodes from the Old Testament, the Cornish dramatist was at least exegetically shrewd and discerning. Had he accomplished nothing more in his efforts at biblical interpretation, he yet would have merited respect for his ability to conceive drama that is both disarmingly straightforward and didactically sound. That he did accomplish more is argument for another chapter.

3. The Legend of the Cross and The Interpretive Frame

SO LONG AS THE drama adheres fairly closely to biblical events, its exegetical implications may justifiably be measured and weighed. When the work swerves from its basic scriptural fidelity, the implications of such an aberration deserve similarly to be measured against what has been seen to be a careful interpretive purpose. The *Origo Mundi* takes just such a turn; and, in the end, the unconventional material illuminates as well as fits the dramatist's exegetical design.

The last incidents of the *Origo Mundi* are centered around the temple, and thereby prefigure the establishment of the church. At the same time the legend of the cross, which has provided a sort of thematic continuity throughout the drama, comes into its own as a central concern. This legend was extremely popular throughout the Middle Ages, and in the *Origo Mundi* it forms a dramatically useful and important bond between several episodes. A careful and thorough study of the origins and development of this legend has yet to be made, but a few preliminary remarks may be offered.

Legendary material that deals with the supposed history of the wood used to build the cross on which Christ was crucified—a history that begins in paradise and finally includes the appearance in the Middle Ages of relics all over Europe—is abundant, contradictory, and confusing. The reasons for the popularity of the legends are not far to seek. The doctrinal importance of the crucifixion made of the cross a ready object of mystical and symbolic veneration. Two ceremonial occasions in the church year are devoted to it: the Feast of the Invention of the Cross, on May 3, celebrates the miraculous finding of the cross in Jerusalem, traditionally in 326, by St. Helena, the mother of Constantine; and the Feast of the Exaltation of the Cross, on September 14, celebrates the consecration, in 335, of the Holy Sepulchre Church in Jerusalem by Bishop Macarius at the order of Constantine, although the popularity of this feast was apparently due to Heraclius' recovery of the relic of the cross from the Persians, in 628.

The significant events commemorated in these church festivals prepared for the gradual dispersion of relics from this consecrated wood. Cornwall was not without a fabulous example of this activity, for there exists a report describing the theft of a piece of the cross by a Cornish knight named Sir Roger de Wallysborough, who managed marvelously to secrete the fragment in his thigh and transport it to Cornwall, where he again marvelously retrieved it. Subsequently, he gave part of the fragment to the parish church at Grade, familiarly known as "crosse parysshe," and part to St. Buryan's, in which district his lands lay.[1] In the late nineteenth century M. Charles Rohault de Fleury listed and discussed some fifteen other surviving relics of the cross in England.[2]

The ceremony of the veneration or adoration of the cross is, furthermore, an important and striking part of the Good Friday liturgy of the Western Church. In this ceremony, commonly called "creeping to the cross," the cross, which has been draped in black, or sometimes purple, is uncovered in stages to the accompaniment of the thrice-uttered priestly proclamation "Ecce lignum crucis, in qua salus nostra pependit" (Behold the wood of the cross, on which our salvation hung), whereupon the clergy—and often the laymen —who are present approach the cross and at three points in their progress genuflect and kiss the earth in veneration.[3] The ceremony apparently began at Jerusalem as early as the fourth century, when, according to the devout lady who set down an account of Christian rites observed then at the Holy City in a document known as *Peregrinatio Etheriae,* a part of the True Cross was exposed to pilgrims for adoration on Good Friday.[4] The ceremony probably accompanied the dispersal of the relics of the cross throughout Europe, and it became so widespread that by the seventh or eighth century it was in general use.[5] This ceremony exemplifies as well the vitality of the emblem as, in Fowler's words, the "dramatic instinct in the Church." [6]

In addition, the cross was important in those quasi-dramatic scenes associated with the liturgy, the *depositio* on Good Friday— sometimes immediately following the ceremony of adoration—together with the *elevatio* on Easter Sunday, which recalls the easy absorption of the symbol into the drama as well as the liturgy of the church. Although according to the various rites both the cross and the Host were used, sometimes alone and sometimes together, in the ritual re-enactment of the burial and resurrection of Christ, Brooks points out that both were used in the Sarum rite and at Exeter, whereas no evidence survives in England to indicate that the Host was ever buried alone.[7]

The legend of the cross as it appears in the *Ordinalia* is, in the main, quite similar to the Latin form of the legend, called from its first words *Post peccatum Adae,* the appearance of which in manuscripts all over Europe indicates its widespread popularity.[8] The legend connects the fatal tree in paradise with the cross of Christ's crucifixion. The links in the chain include an old and traditional story, found most notably perhaps in the apocryphal *Gospel of Nicodemus,* of the quest of Seth for the "oil of mercy," together with several patriarchal figures and events out of the Old Testament, as well as a curious prechristian martyrdom and prophecy.

As the legend unfolds in the *Origo Mundi,* Adam sends his son Seth, who was born after Cain murdered Abel, to paradise for

the "oil of mercy" that God had promised at the expulsion from
the garden of Eden. Seth returns with three pips from the apple
"a dybrys adam the das" (which Adam, thy father, ate: *OM* 824),
having been directed to place them under Adam's tongue at his
burial. He carries out the request, and the seeds develop eventually
into three sprouts that Moses finds, recognizes as a type of the
trinity, cuts, and finally plants on Mount Tabor. David is directed
in a dream to find and bring them to Jerusalem. He locates the
"rods" and brings them to Jerusalem, where they miraculously take
root overnight as a single tree, under which David is later sitting
when he decides to build the temple. Later, Solomon desires the
tree for the central beam in the temple; but it magically resists all
the carpenters' efforts to fit it into place, and is therefore placed
within the temple as an object of veneration. A girl named Maximilla enters, sits on the beam, and suddeny finds her clothing afire,
whereupon she successfully and amazingly invokes the aid of Christ.
The bishop overhears this idolatrous invocation and promptly con-
demns her to a martyr's death, further directing that the offensive
beam be removed to the pool Bethsaida. There, however, it continues to work miracles of healing, an alarming habit that moves the
splenetic bishop finally to have it placed as a footbridge over the
"brook Cedron," where it reposes until required for the crucifixion.

The development of the legend has not yet adequately been
traced. One form of the legend utterly ignores the pre-Mosaic parts
of the story and generally diverges thereafter, which led Napier to
conclude that two fundamentally varying legends developed "from
some common source." [9]

The most striking feature of the cross legend is its incorporation with the very old legend of Seth and his quest for the oil of
mercy. This tale, most recently studied by Miss Quinn,[10] was drawn
from a first century Jewish writing, the *Apocalypse of Moses,* the
Latin version of which is known as the *Vita Adae et Evae,* for
inclusion in the possibly fifth century second part, or "Descent

into Hell," of the *Gospel of Nicodemus*.[11] In this late Christian apocryphal writing, known also as the *Acta Pilati,* two men who had been raised from the dead at the resurrection of Jesus, Karinus and Leucius, report their experiences to the Jewish elders. The story they tell is the basis for the popular patristic and medieval legend of the Harrowing of Hell: at a premonition of the divine assault about to be made on the infernal citadel to which they have been consigned, the patriarchs and prophets describe in turn their several expectations of the redeemer. Isaiah, Simeon, and John the Baptist recall their prophecies; then Adam asks his son Seth to "declare unto thy sons the patriarchs and the prophets all that thou didst hear from Michael the archangel, when I sent thee unto the gates of paradise that thou mightest entreat God to send thee his angel to give thee the oil of the tree of mercy." [12] Thereupon Seth supplies the kernel of the material that was to become a full-fledged visit to and vision of the terrestrial paradise.

Miss Quinn suggests that at some point, perhaps as early as the *Vita Adae et Evae,* the oil that had been the "link and the symbol connecting the Seth legend and Christianity," gave way to the wood.[13] Although, to be sure, the formula used by Seth in the *Gospel of Nicodemus* is the "oil of the tree of mercy," [14] no explanation of the merging of the symbols is attempted. In fact, the archangel promises that in the fullness of time, "the Son of God [shall] come upon the earth to raise up the body of Adam and the bodies of the dead, and he shall . . . anoint with the oil of mercy all that believe on him," [15] whereas subsequently the triumphant Jesus exhorts those whom, without unction, he has liberated: "Ye that by the tree and the devil and death were condemned, behold now the devil and death condemned by the tree." [16] Indeed, a satisfactory resolution of the dilemma posed by two interchangeable symbols—the oil and the wood—is never really apparent, for the *oleum misericordiae,* once a strong symbol in its own right,[17] simply becomes a verbal symbol, once removed, almost a euphemism. As for the wood, the iconographic tree of Jesse, a popular subject in medieval church art, suggests itself as a possible source or analogue, if not of the tree in paradise, at least of the attempt to associate the wood with several patriarchal generations. Even so, no satisfactory evidence supports such a hypothesis.[18]

The first securely attested connection of the legend of Seth's quest for the oil of mercy with the legendary history of the cross is a brief description by Johannes Beleth, in his *Rationale divinorum officiorum,* about 1170,[19] deriving from his explanation of the feast of the Exaltation of the Cross. The body of the legend remains to be filled in, and even Jacobus de Voragine, in his celebrated and widely popular *Legenda aurea* (ca. 1266), skips hastily from Seth's mission to the building of the temple under Solomon.

Nevertheless, the legend was in fact refined and elaborated so that finally the story of the cross was sustained historically from Seth's return out of paradise to the crucifixion. In this form, described above as the legend *Post peccatum Adae,* the mythic history of the cross was popular and was thought important enough to deserve its own place in a number of manuscripts.[20] It was part of the standard repertoire on which commentators, homilists, teachers, and rhetoricians customarily drew. Among English vernacular writings, it occurs both in the *Southern Legendary* [21] and in the *Northern Passion,*[22] in Mirk's *Festial,*[23] in *Cursor Mundi,*[24] and in *Canticum Creatione.*[25]

Like *Cursor Mundi,* which has inappropriately been suggested as its source,[26] the *Ordinalia* has broken up the legend and incorporated its materials smoothly into the scriptural matter drawn from the Old Testament. This episodic treatment begins after Abel's murder, when Adam and Eve are instructed to give birth to another son, Seth, whom Adam, approaching death, sends for the oil of mercy promised at his expulsion from paradise (*OM* 325–330).

At this point the Cornish play reads almost like a dramatized paraphrase of the Latin version of the legend, for it does not deviate

DUQUESNE UNIVERSITY LIBRARY 891.622 O65

from *Post peccatum Adae,* and there are even some notable verbal
parallels. In Seth's first description of what he has seen, for example, the drama reads,

> ol an tekter a wylys
> ny yl taves den yn bys
> y leuerel bynytha.

(The tongue of no man in the world can ever describe all the
beauty that I saw: *OM* 764–766.) The Latin text, by comparison,
has "tantam intuitus est amenitatem, quam lingua humana enodare
non posset." "Frut da ha floures tek/menestrouthy ha can whek"
(good fruit and fair flowers, minstrelsy and sweet song: *OM* 769–
770) is very close to the "fructum florum cum armonia avium";
and the "fenten bryght Avel arhans" (fountain bright as silver:
OM 771) is not an unlikely rendering of the "fontem lucidissi-
mum." Indeed, the correspondence between the Cornish play and
Latin legend is textually helpful in this episode. Norris' emendation,
removing the lines numbered in his edition *OM* 781–788 from
their position in the manuscript after line 808, however understandable, is unnecessary and unjustifiable, since the dramatist's
fidelity to the Latin legend, where the description of the roots of
the tree follows Seth's third look into paradise, indicates the impropriety of the alteration.

The dramatist omits a few of the details given in the Latin
legend: for example, Seth does not name the four rivers—"pedyr
streyth" (*OM* 772)—that flow from the fountain in paradise, nor
does he see the soul of his brother Abel in hell where the roots of
the tree penetrate, nor does he make the observation that the tree
is without bark or leaves because of his parents' sin ("arborem
illam esse nudatam propter peccata [parentum]"). Nonetheless,
the dramatist keeps, if he does not in fact strengthen, the soteriological emphasis of the episode when he has the angel assure Seth
not only that the new-born child he has seen among the branches of
the tree is the Son of God and the oil of mercy by which Adam and

his posterity will be redeemed, but also that this redemption will
come by the death of the child:

> dre y vernans yredy
> ol an bys a fyth sylwys.

(Through his death, clearly all the world will be saved: *OM* 817–
818.) The dramatist also has the commendable restraint to omit
one of the least digestible extravagances of the legend, a tradition
according to which there grew from the seeds of the apple that
Adam had eaten three or four kinds of tree—cedar, cypress, pine,
and sometimes olive.

The episode, like the legend that is its source, includes a great
deal of incompletely absorbed or blended material, but the dramatist has not apparently been so concerned with the symbolic significance of the separate parts as with the dramatic effect of the whole
episode. The burned footprints he partially explains, after his
source, as the result of the very plants' refusal to grow in the steps
of the fallen sinners as they had left paradise (*OM* 711–715). One
is tempted to speculate on the symbolic significance of the dry tree
itself, the serpent and the child in it, the geography of paradise, the
three trips that Seth makes in order to look into the garden. Such
problems have been discussed elsewhere,[27] however, and I am
hesitant, on the grounds of slight evidence, to speculate about the
extent of the dramatist's awareness of such symbolic subtleties in
his material.

The concept of the return to paradise, on the other hand,
clearly has some importance for the drama. If the expulsion was, as
Irenaeus insists, in a sense an act of mercy, since it permitted death
finally to put an end to man's sin,[28] then a return to paradise and to
the untainted mercy that it represents is understandably a desirable
spiritual venture. The terrestrial paradise endures therefore not
merely as an eschatological, but also as a pre-eschatological hope.[29]
It was a natural symbol for the mystics, who strove for spiritual
perfection,[30] and some germ of this mystical longing is possibly

present in the Cornish plays. Miss Quinn suggests that baptismal typology may also be involved in this return to paradise, but the correspondence is more applicable to the quest of Seth before than after it becomes attached to the legend of the cross, and is probably strongest so long as it remains associated with the descent into hell and the *Gospel of Nicodemus*.[31] Indeed, far more important than any such conceptual symbolism is the metaphorical power that the dramatist achieves by so palpably connecting the crucifixion and the fall. This idea is, of course, a very old one: "The trespass which came by the tree was undone by the tree of obedience, when, hearkening unto God, the Son of Man was nailed to the tree." [32] And in a moral sense, St. Bonaventure contrasts the *lignum vitae* and the *lignum vetiti*.[33] What for the dramatist is most useful and significant is the visual and representational power of making the cross a seedling from the tree by which came death, and the vitality of this perception grows increasingly clear throughout the drama.

As the angel had predicted, Adam dies three days after Seth returns from his mission. Seth plants the seeds given him by the angel under his father's tongue, from which they grow [34] to the three *guelen* (*virgulae*) or twigs discovered, after the flood, by Moses. The association of both Moses and David with the legend is a relatively late, although not at all an illogical, development. Had the legend continued to develop, in fact, other incidents and other patriarchs would no doubt have appeared in it.

After the crossing of the Red Sea, the dramatic treatment of Moses in the *Ordinalia* is closely modeled on the Latin legend. Even the curious and otherwise inexplicable (since neither biblical nor traditional) decision, in which Joshua, Caleb, and Moses participate, to build dwellings—*castel, ostel, chy,* and *scovva*—immediately after their miraculous crossing, is drawn from the statement in the Latin legend: "venit in Ebron, ubi cum castra metatus fuisset Moyses, in uespera sanctificato populo tres virgulae quae stabant in ore Adae apparuerunt" (They came to Hebron, where in the evening, after Moses had laid out their camp, the three twigs that had grown from the mouth of [the dead] Adam appeared to the chosen people). And, to be sure, the rods are promptly discovered, and Moses properly observes them to be a type of the Trinity.[35] The episodes of water elicited from the rock, the burial of the rods, and the death of Moses follow in swift succession.

The inclusion at this point of the biblical incident of the water drawn from a rock is not surprising. Indeed, the episode helps to make clear the general relationship of the legend to biblical exegesis while it throws light as well on the particular aims of the Cornish dramatist. The account of this event used by the legend is roughly a paraphrase of the biblical story narrated in Numbers 20:1-13.

Legend

Contigit autem ad contradictionis aquas, cum filii Israel jurgarentur contra dominum et contra Moisen, in ira locutus est Moises dicens: Audite, rebelles et increduli! Numquid poterimus vobis eicere aquam de petra hac? Et percutiens bis silicem virga egressae sunt aquae largissimae, ita ut biberent populi et jumenta.

Facto miraculo apparuit dominus Moysi dicens: Quia non sanctificasti nomen meum coram filiis Israel, non introduces populum hunc in terram promissionis.

Cui Moises ait: Miserere mei, Domine! Quis ergo, domine, eos introducet? Cui dominus ait: Vivat dominus! nullus eorum ingredietur terram promissionis praeter Calef et Josue.

Bible

Haec est aqua contradictionis, ubi jurgati sunt filii Israel contra Dominum. [verse 13]

Dixitque eis: Audite, rebelles et increduli: Num de petra hac vobis aquam poterimus ejicere? Cumque elevasset Moyses manum, percutiens virga bis silicem, egressae sunt aquae largissimae, ita ut populus biberet et jumenta. [verses 10–11]

Dixitque Dominus ad Moysen et Aaron: Quia non credidistis mihi, ut sanctificaretis me coram filiis Israel, non introducetis hos populos in terram, quam dabo eis. [verse 12]

(Legend: Yet it happened, at the water of contradiction, when the children of Israel quarreled against the Lord and against Moses, Moses spoke in wrath, saying: Hear, ye rebels and unbelievers! Can we bring you forth water out of this rock? And when he struck the rock twice with the rod, there came forth water in great abundance, so that the people and their cattle drank.

(When the miracle had been wrought, the Lord appeared to Moses, saying: because you did not sanctify my name before the children of Israel, you may not bring these people into the promised land.

(To which Moses said: Have mercy on me, Lord. Who, then, O Lord, may lead them? To which the Lord said: As the Lord lives, none of them may enter the promised land except Caleb and Joshua.

(Bible: This is the water of contradiction, where the children of Israel strove with words against the Lord. [13]

(He said to them: Hear, ye rebellious and incredulous: Can we bring you forth water out of this rock? And when Moses had lifted up his hand, and struck the rock twice with the rod, there came forth water in great abundance, so that the people and their cattle drank. And the Lord said to Moses and Aaron: Because you have not believed me, to sanctify me before the children of Israel, you shall not bring these people into the land, which I will give them. [10-12; Douay version])

The Cornish dramatist probably had before him this version of the story from the Latin legend,[36] since he concludes the episode with the same colloquy between God and Moses, which he virtually translates and versifies:

> wheth ol bywe y a wra
> nyns a den vyth vynytha
>   a'n keth re-na the'n tyr sans
> marnas calef ha iosue.

(Of all those [that] are yet living, not any man of them shall ever go to the holy land, except Caleb and Joshua: *OM* 1877–1880.) The dramatist, however, is characteristically even more reliant on the biblical account of the episode, for he carefully includes Aaron in Moses' deliberations about what is to be done, and in general his elaborations expand the brief legendary account by paraphrasing the scriptural account; he uses, in fact, the significant and striking phrase *aquae vivae:*

> a das dev y'th wolowys
> clew galow a'n bobyl-ma
> dour may fens y dysehys
> a vevnans re dethe gura.

(O father, God, in thy light, hear the call of this people: that they may be refreshed, give to them the water of life: *OM* 1831–1834.) [37] The use of this phrase is typologically important, for Paul himself related this event to baptism and identified the rock with Christ (1 Corinthians 10:1–4). The parallel with the episode at the crucifixion, treated in the *Ordinalia* (PC 3003–3030), in which a blind man thrusts a spear into Christ's side and has his sight restored by the blood which flows thence, is obvious. On the other hand, as the use of the episode in the legend indicates, if the rock typifies Christ and if the waters represent the regenerative powers of his spilt blood (symbolized in the baptismal water, the *aquae vitae*), then the rod is in some sense prefigurative not only of the blind man's spear but also of the cross, in whose history the legend overtly places this episode.

In fact, the liturgical custom whereby the "wood of the cross" is plunged into the baptismal waters at their consecration, although principally thought to be derived from the tree (*lignum*) with which Moses sweetened the bitter waters of Marah,[38] nonetheless indicates the strong iconographical identification of this dramatic event with the crucifixion and with the rite of baptism; so strong, indeed, that an illustration in one thirteenth century French manuscript depicts Moses' rod in the shape of a cross.[39]

On the other hand, the Cornish dramatist never resolves the confusion that arises in this episode between the talismanic rod that Moses received at his first meeting with God (*OM* 1447–1461), and these rods, which he found later. In the Latin legend the confusion does not arise because the former rod is not introduced. Whether from bafflement or for intentional ambiguity, the dramatist has ignored the problem.

There is a curious similarity between the miracles effected by the legendary three rods after Moses' discovery and the biblical miracles wrought by the bronze serpent, which Moses erected on a pole in order that people who had been bitten by serpents might, by looking on it, be restored (Numbers 21:6–9). According to the legend, "cumque aliqui in exercitu percussi a serpentibus uel ab aliis uermibus uenenosis veniebant ad prophetam, deosculantes uirgulas sanabantur" (Whenever anyone in the army who had been stung by serpents or other poisonous reptiles came to the prophet [Moses], they were healed by kissing the rods). In the *Ordinalia* Moses uses the rods themselves to cure poisoning. The connection is not unnatural, for the bronze serpent was regarded as another of the typological foreshadowings of Christ, after the comparison in the gospel: "And as Moses lifted up the serpent in the wilderness, even so must the Son of man be lifted up" (John 3:14–15). Furthermore, although of more doubtful validity, the curious serpent wrapped about the tree in Seth's vision of paradise is worthy of recall (*OM* 797). If the Cornish dramatist is aware of any such similarities, he does not indicate it, however, and here as elsewhere he appears to be faithful to the legend.[40]

The episodes that deal with David are again taken sequentially from the usual form of the Latin legend, although the Cornish dramatist embellishes most of the scenes to fit his purposes. He goes to the biblical account for the king's affair with Bathsheba, an episode to which the legend alludes only in passing: "post peccatum grande [or *grave*], quod commiserat David" (after the great sin that David committed). Other elaborations emphasize the courtly splendor that befits a king, as when David's butler succors him with fine wine and wraps him in rich cloth as he naps; still others afford some of the relatively rare occasions for comic byplay in the drama, as when the guardians of the rods exchange lecherous pleasantries and when David employs a messenger to round up masons for building the temple, for which services the messenger is suitably awarded the baronial rights to some local Cornish lands.

The Davidic episodes in the *Ordinalia* diverge from the Latin legend principally in giving to Gabriel rather than to David himself the prophecy of the crucifixion, and in introducing the healing of a blind man, a lame man, and a deaf man through the efficacy of the marvelous "rods." On this point, to be sure, there is a good deal of variation in the manuscripts of the Latin legend. While Meyer's text only suggests that healing took place,[41] Suchier's lists specifically those who are leprous, feverish, blind, and deaf.[42] The "Rood-tree group" generally have three miracles at this point, in which first a rich man is healed, then three black men are made white, and finally a leper is restored.[43] The confusion indicates that the dramatist or his source either amplified the brief *salvabantur* or attempted to reconcile the varying accounts. At any rate, the three miracles prescribed in the *Ordinalia* were ready at hand in the messianic prophecy of Isaiah (35:5–6): "then the eyes of the blind shall be opened, and the ears of the deaf shall be unstopped. Then shall the lame man leap as an hart." The healing is "dre grath a'n gueel" (by the grace of the rods: *OM* 2019), and David pronounces the liturgical formula "in nomine patris et filii, atque spiritus sancti" (*OM* 2020–2021). This particular anachronism is probably due to the dramatist's endeavor to deal with the assertion in the legend that by these healings, David "intellexit . . . misterium sanctae crucis" (understood the mystery of the holy cross).[44] The legend again, and the dramatist after it, is at pains to make clear by these prefigurative miracles that the cross is itself an agent, and not merely a symbol, of the mercy that is to come.

The concluding episodes in the prechristian history cluster about the person of Solomon. The principal occasion dramatized in the *Ordinalia* is the prophecy and martyrdom of the mysterious Maximilla. The association of Solomon with the cross may seem perplexing, and Quinn misleadingly suggests that "Solomon, as the

great Jewish king and builder of the Temple, symbolizes Judaism.
In his failure to recognize the unique nature and destiny of the
wood, he prefigured the failure of the Jews to recognize the Mes-
siah." [45] In point of fact, Solomon, far from failing to recognize
the uniqueness of the wood, has it put into the temple as an object
of veneration: "Hoc miraculo viso [the tree's refusal to accom-
modate the carpenters' measurements], precepit Salomon ut in
templo poneretur et ab universis introeuntibus honoraretur"
(Having seen this miracle, Solomon ordered that it be placed in
the temple and that it be honored by all who should enter there).[46]
All the versions agree on this point, and the *Ordinalia* makes it
even more emphatically than most. Apropos of the tree, King Solomon instructs the carpenters:

> my a comonnd y wore
>   gans enour bras desympys
> yn temple the wrowethe,
> ha guetyeugh pup y worthye
>   war beyn agas bos lethys.

(I command you forthwith to put it, with great honour to lie in the
temple, and take care all to worship it on pain that you be killed:
OM 2552–2556.) The death of Maximilla and the further humilia-
tions visited on the wood of the cross are, in fact, instigated by the
"bishop" of the temple, who, though appointed by Solomon as a
reward for his faithful counsel, is rather a type of that later and in-
famous ecclesiastic "bishop" Caiaphas, while Solomon himself is a
reverential patriarch in the manner of Moses and David.

Solomon's role in the legend may be clarified somewhat by a
couple of difficult biblical passages. In the *Canticum Canticorum
Salomonis* there is a description of Solomon's litter (*lectulum
Salomonis*), in which his beloved travels "sicut virgula fumi ex
aromatibus myrrhae . . . Ferculum fecit sibi rex Salomon de lignis
Libani; columnas ejus fecit argenteas . . . media charitate constravit propter filias Jerusalem" (as a pillar of smoke of aromatic
spices . . . King Solomon hath made him a litter of the wood of

Libanus: the pillars thereof he made of silver . . . the midst he covered with charity for the daughters of Jerusalem: Canticles 3:6–10).[47] A number of coincidental characteristics are to be remarked in the treatment of the wood of the cross: the twigs are invariably observed to emit a sweet odor; at David's direction silver rings are set about the tree to mark its yearly growth; and when Maximilla enters the temple, her dress catches fire as she sits on the venerable beam—when, so to speak, she treats it as a litter.

The connection is reinforced by a New Testament allusion to this passage. As Jesus carried the cross toward the crucifixion, he addressed the weeping women: "Daughters of Jerusalem, weep not for me, but weep for yourselves, and for your children . . . For if they do these things in a green tree, what shall be done in the dry?" (Luke 23:28–31). William Durandus no doubt has this relationship in mind when, in discussing church symbolism, he quotes a fragment of the passage from the Canticles: "Crux triumphalis, in plurisque locis, in medio ecclesiae ponitur, ad notandum quod de medio corde Redemptorem nostrum diligimus, qui, juxta Salomonem, corpus suum *media charitate constravit propter filias Hierusalem,* et ut omnes signum victoriae videntes, dicant: Ave salus totius saeculi, arbor salutifera." (The triumphal cross, in the majority of places, is set in the midst of the church, signifying that we love our Redeemer from the midst of our hearts, for he, like Solomon, 'covered the midst' of his body 'with charity for the daughters of Jerusalem,' and in order that all who see the sign of victory may say: Hail, salvation of all the world, O tree that bears salvation.) [48] In effect, the *Canticum Canticorum* was traditionally regarded, in its purported celebration of the wedding of Solomon and his beloved, as prophetic of the relationship between Christ and the church.[49] It is not accidental that the cross is essential to this union, and it is therefore understandable that, as a type of the church, Solomon would have the wood of the cross venerated in his temple.

Maximilla is the woman—sometimes a strumpet [50]—who suffers martyrdom as a result of calling on the name of Jesus for aid when her clothes are miraculously set afire after she sits on the beam that is destined to become the wood of the cross. She is also an indeterminate figure. In most forms of the Latin legend the episode of Maximilla's proto-martyrdom is followed by a prophecy of the Queen of Sheba, who, coming to try the wisdom of Solomon, refuses to walk over a bridge above the brook Cedron, because she recognizes in its wood the sanctity of the cross.[51] The *Ordinalia* does not include this latter episode, possibly because the dramatist or his source recognized the fundamental similarity between it and the Maximilla story.

Miss Quinn suggests, it seems to me rightly, that the two episodes probably derive from a single prototype.[52] Both can probably be linked to the popular notion that the old Sybilline oracles, like Virgil, were prechristian, non-biblical prophets of Christ.[53] It is not unlikely that the name "Maximilla" represents a contraction of the epithet and name *maxima sybilla,*[54] and in the various forms of the legend other names are given, such as "Queen Sivila," [55] "Sibilla," [56] "Maxilla," [57] and "Marsobilia." [58] In the Holy Rood-tree version of the legend, as Miss Quinn points out, the harlot quotes a prophecy from the Sybilline Oracles when her clothes are burnt.[59]

For the purposes of the drama, it is simply helpful to notice that this martyrdom suffered on account of the holy wood makes dramatically complete both the legendary material and the exegetical method itself. In the girl's martyrdom, the mercy, the wood of the cross, and the name of Jesus are finally associated, and the forces of evil prevail. The legend is poised for its climax in the crucifixion; the drama prepares thematically for the redemption. The Old Testament material is preliminary, and its work is to justify the culmination of the drama: the concept of the fall, the exegetical typology, and the affirmation of a historical process are essential parts of the realization of that purpose, and the legend serves them all. Although the *Ordinalia* suffers in many ways from dramatic immaturity, the incorporation of this legend of the cross into the conventional patriarchal and prechristian material is itself a masterly dramatic stroke, and one can only wonder that it was not subsequently imitated.[60]

The *Origo Mundi,* after the martyrdom of Maximilla, disposes of its little unfinished dramatic business by moving the cross from the temple to the pool of Bethsaida, which was the site of a miraculous healing later by Jesus (John 5:1–9); and from there to the brook Cedron (*OM* 2783, 2804–2815). This procedure, again, conforms to the Latin legend. It may be observed in passing that the names of the men who carry the cross about are themselves taken from the Old Testament language of hostility, for Gebal and Amalek were part of a confederacy of nations united against Israel (Psalms 83:8).

The precise significance of the legend for the *Ordinalia* is finally a delicate matter. One scholar has written about the various forms of the legend that "they are nothing more than what we have called the ancient Christian mystery of the cross that has here been naively remoulded by the artistry of folklore and so made vivid to men's minds. At the back of this proliferation of tales is the purely theological conviction that Christ and Adam, the pneumatic and the fleshly man, are intimately linked together (cf. 1 Cor. 15. 45–49), and while these legends are passed on by whispered word-of-mouth and by pictorial imagery, the clear, sharply defined formulations of ancient theology continue down the centuries. Thus the classical antithesis is kept alive by which the wood of Paradise is brought into relation with the wood of the cross." [61]

If the "classical antithesis" between Christ and Adam, the "purely theological conviction" that the mystery of the cross links man's fall with his redemption, are indisputably at the basis of the legend's vitality, nonetheless the growth of the legend, its increasing popularity in exegesis as well as in story, and finally, for present purposes, its skillful incorporation by the Cornish artist into the changing scenes of his drama point to another, more subtle, less clearly symbolic role. The use of the cross within the exegetical pattern of the Old Testament is at least a first step toward combining biblical and legendary material in a common typological frame. The legend establishes a palpable dramatic bond between the events of the first day's play and the events of the plays that follow. Furthermore, this bond manifests in the *Ordinalia* the essential historical concern behind all medieval biblical drama. Its dilemma, and the dilemma of all apologists for the Christian view of history, is to make intelligible a historical process that is at once literally sequential and mystically christocentric. Christian exegesis developed, to explain the paradox, a method that attempts basically to distinguish between an event and its implications. The legend of the cross is useful to the dramatist for the same methodological reasons. The three pips that Seth brings back from paradise have a linear history of their own, the development of which binds several episodes precariously together. The pips, the rods, the tree, the beam, and finally the cross itself, however, at all times mystically embody the promised "oil of mercy," and their appearance repeatedly manifests this inward grace. Christ himself, as becomes explicit in the Harrowing of Hell, is effectively the "oil of mercy." The events of the legend are thus dramatically emblematic of the historical and therefore exegetical significance of man's experience between the fall and the redemption.

The problem of exegesis in the rest of the drama, which treats the life of Christ from the temptation to the ascension, is largely a part of problems treated elsewhere in this study—chiefly, the matter of the doctrinal ideas that contribute to the christology of the play. The principal questions that may properly engage our attention at this point are: What scriptural material has the dramatist omitted? On what basis has he chosen the material that he includes? What non-scriptural matter is in the plays, from what sources, and for what reasons? Finally, how, specifically, has the dramatist organized his material?

The nativity is the most surprising omission from the subjects treated in the *Ordinalia*. This omission can be explained liturgically, since in the church year the emphasis on the patriarchal prefiguration of Christ falls after Christmas and immediately before Lent; and doctrinally, since the mystery of the incarnation unfolds gradually and climactically in the drama. Yet dramatically, it is more difficult to understand, since the nativity plays were so evidently popular elsewhere in the medieval theater. Once again, however, the dramatic coherence of the *Ordinalia* asserts itself. In a more episodic drama the nativity scenes would be a high point; the Cornish *Ordinalia,* however, episodic though in many respects it indeed is, steadfastly moves toward a sustained doctrinal and dramatic climax. The transition from episode to episode is not always very smooth, but no single incident contrives to dominate the action or to impede the dramatic momentum toward the redemption. This omission is, in other words, exegetically insignificant. Only dramatically is it remarkable. On the one hand, as McNeir rightly observes, if the plays "had not been effective as drama, they would have failed in their aim of religious instruction;" [62] on the other hand, the dramatic form had to fit the doctrinal matter, as well. The *Ordinalia* seldom sacrifices its principal doctrinal intentions for ephemeral dramatic effect.

If the nativity is remarkable for its absence from the *Ordinalia,* the inclusion of the *Mors Pilati* is no less noteworthy. This story of the curing and conversion of the Emperor Tiberius at the hands of Veronica, and their subsequent joint revenge upon Pilate, whose death and damnation follows, is clumsily inserted whole into the *Resurrexio Domini* between the last scene pertinent to the resurrection—the persuasion of the doubting apostle Thomas that Jesus had indeed risen—and the portrayal of the ascension. Dramatically, the story is an intrusion; its crude motif of revenge interrupts the treatment of the glorification of the Redeemer, and it suddenly shifts the sights of the play from the work of Christ to hagiography, even though in the last scene the focus begins to slip back. What vengeance the redemptive theme requires is theological and is adequately treated in the Harrowing of Hell. By no doctrinal or dramatic standards, in effect, can the Death of Pilate be seen as other than an interruption.

This difficulty seems to have troubled the scribes who worked over the manuscript, for, as at no other point in the drama, Latin directions have been inserted before and after the episode to set it off firmly from the rest of the work.[63] Although supporting evidence is wanting to give credence to the opinion, it seems doubtful that the *Mors Pilati* was part of the *Ordinalia* as originally conceived. Where the legend of the cross and other non-biblical material was worked into the very fabric of the drama, this story is dropped awkwardly and unassimilably into the last day's play. If the episode was not added by a later editorial hand, the dramatist showed an uncharacteristic ineptitude by including it as it stands.

The story itself is an entertaining, though relatively late, legend that sometimes occurs as an appendix to the *Gospel of Nicodemus* —it is so treated by James [64]—and was popular enough to have been included in the *Legenda aurea* [65] and in Ranulph Higden's *Polychronicon*.[66] The *Gospel of Nicodemus* itself was popular, and is ultimately the source of the episode of Christ's descent into hell after his crucifixion. In light of the Cornish dramatist's treatment of this famous Harrowing of Hell, he may be presumed to have known the *Gospel* itself, although his source for the episode may just as likely have been one of the versified versions or even an independent dramatic version of the traditional story.[67]

The Cornish dramatist has also drawn on material from the *Gospel of Nicodemus* in his use of the legend of Longinus, although the particular emphases in the drama indicate familiarity with other late and popular medieval versions of the story. In the *Ordinalia,* Longius (as he is named) is a blind man whose sight miraculously returns when his eyes are touched by the blood flowing from the wound that his spear thrust has opened in Christ's side. While the legend occurs regularly in the cycle plays, the Cornish dramatist's treatment is modest and unembroidered. As Miss Peebles has pointed out in her study of the legend, such a presentation is more consonant with later English than with continental models, where Longinus is usually a much more involved and frequently a humorous character.[68] Miss Wright, on the other hand, is inclined to rely heavily on a similarity in this episode to support her opinion that the French *Passion d'Arras* may have been the source of the Cornish plays or that the two plays may have had a common source.[69] There are verbal similarities, but a far more cautious comparison is in order. For the French play gives nearly six times as many octosyllabic lines to the episode as the Cornish play, and the *Passion d'Arras* generally is vastly more diffuse than the *Ordinalia*. Here, as always, a certain perspective is valuable. Speculation about French affinities is attractive enough, but substantial evidence of kinship requires a more extensive foundation than an occasional biological similarity permits. On balance, Miss Peebles' seems the more sober and is certainly the more conservative view.

Another of the interesting non-biblical materials incorporated into the story of Christ's passion is the odd incident of the smith who, upon being asked to fashion the nails for the cross, refuses and miraculously contracts leprosy to justify his refusal to the executioners (*PC* 2670–2736). His wife then proceeds to work the forge effectively in his behalf. This story of the smith and his hardy dame occurs also in the *Northern Passion* [70] and in nearly all the French passion plays,[71] and is a theme in medieval art.[72] The scene certainly foreshadows the stock character of the shrew that became quite popular in the dramatic cycles, although in the Cornish play the smith and his woman may in a small way be intended, on the verge of the crucifixion, to recall as well the folly of the first woman.

In addition to these specific scenes, drawn from legendary and apocryphal sources, the biblical matter was reinforced by liturgical and hymnodic echoes, as well as by religious poetry, the most notable use of which occurs in the thrice-repeated lament of the three Marys at the tomb. This striking couplet, first uttered or sung in English and then paraphrased in Cornish, has no known prototype.[73] I suspect, in fact, that the whole brief but very moving interlude, during which the English lines are used as a refrain, may be a paraphrase or translation of a lost English poem. The English verses run as follows:

> ellas mornyngh y syngh mornyng y cal
> our lord ys deyd that bogthe ovs al.

(*RD* 733–734, 753–754, 779–780.)

The dramatist's characteristic indulgence in farcical, even mordant, byplay on the part of the torturers, executioners, and jailers has its source everywhere and nowhere, for the medieval plays abound in it, and their audiences may be presumed to have enjoyed it, though modern sensibilities are unable to explain or understand it.[74] On the other hand, the dramatist is able demonstrably and effectively to transcend both his material and sources to make so moving a dramatic point as in his treatment of the apostle Thomas' doubts. This incident was also quite popular in the Middle Ages: the tympanum of the church of St. Thomas at Strasbourg, for example, has a relief that shows Christ guiding Thomas' hands to his open wounds, and there are "cycles" devoted to the apostle in stained glass at Bourges, Chartres, Tours, and Assisi.[75] The achievement of the Cornish dramatist lies in his appropriate use of Thomas' insistent but sorrowful incredulity and its triumphal resolution in a chastened but solid faith as the climax of his drama. The informing theme of the drama is the redemption. The resurrection proclaims it, the descent into hell confirms it, and the series of appearances to the faithful, culminating in Thomas' agonized progress to faith, fulfills it. Dramatically, the episode is the finest in the *Ordinalia*.

The drama ends, appropriately, with the ascension. Few scenes in the Cornish plays lend themselves so well to a careful study of the characteristic dramatic usage of sources, themes, and techniques. The ascension begins with a colloquy between Jesus and his disciples that draws on the "high-priestly prayer" in chapter 17 of the gospel of John—where it precedes the crucifixion—and the various charges to "go into all the world and preach." [76]

For the ascension itself, there was chiefly available the biblical account in Acts 1:6–11. The drama does not make clear or take much interest in the mechanics of the ascension, and it entirely ignores the apostles after Jesus' ascent, although the biblical episode has "two men in white robes" marvelously appear to ask, "Viri Galilaei, quid statis aspicientes in coelum?" (Acts 1:11). The drama rather concentrates on the celestial effect of the ascension.

At the approach of Jesus, the angels begin to ask themselves who the approaching adventurer might be. Their questions are based on the text of Isaiah 63:1–9: "Quis est iste ["pyv henna": *RD* 2487] qui venit de Edom ["henna a edom re thueth": *RD* 2505]? . . . Quare ergo rubrum est indumentum tuum ["pyv a ylta gy bones/ pen yw mar ruth the thylles": *RD* 2511–2512]?" (Who is this that cometh from Edom: . . . Why then is thy apparel red? Douay version.) The passage, which affirms at once the wrath of judgment and the mercy of redemption, occurs in the Benedictine Breviary on the Feast of the Ascension, and is not an unlikely allusion.[77] The red garments are in art the customary garb of Jesus after the resurrection. In the Canticles the "beloved," representing Christ, is described: "Dilectus meus candidus et rubicundus" (My beloved is white and ruddy: 5:10. Douay version). Durandus furthermore observed that "red vestments are used . . . upon the Feast of that Holy Cross, whereon Christ shed His Blood for us; as saith the Prophet, *'Wherefore art Thou red in thine Apparel, like him that treadeth in the Winevat?'* " [78]

The association of Edom with this color and with the ascension is reinforced both by its meaning (red) [79] and its identification, as one of the enemies of Israel, with Jewish messianic and eschatological literature.[80] The implication of the allusion is to battle— indeed, one of the angels describes Christ's rubicund appearance as

> yn ruth,
> avel gos pen ha duscouth,
> garrow ha treys

(red, like blood, head and shoulders, legs and feet: *RD* 2499–2501). The battle imagery recalls the exchanges between Spiritus Christi and Satan at the Harrowing of Hell: "Quis est iste rex

gloriae? Dominus fortis et potens, Dominus potens in proelio"
(Who is this King of Glory? The Lord who is strong and mighty:
the Lord mighty in battle: Psalms 23/24:8). And, indeed, Jesus
finally identifies himself as a warrior.

The motif of Christ the Knight was popular, and in these concluding lines of the *Ordinalia* the image is caught powerfully, as
Jesus describes his battle: the battlefield was the cross; his armor
included thorns for a helmet, nails for gloves and shoes, the bloody
scourges for robe and breastplate (*RD* 2571–2606).[81] The symbols
of the passion are called "þese armus of crist boþ god and man"
in the meditative verse printed by Morris,[82] and the idea is remotely
reminiscent of Paul's use of similar imagery to describe "the whole
armor of God" (Ephesians 6:10–17). The violent imagery of the
Apocalypse reinforces it, and the general attitude of hostility that
was thought to exist between God and the devil is, of course, everywhere in the thought and literature of the church: "The Word
Incarnate is our King," writes Hugh of St. Victor, "who came into
the world to fight the devil; all the saints who were before his coming are as soldiers going before the royal presence; those who came
after, and those to come, until the end of the world, are as soldiers
following the King. And the King is in the midst of his army." [83]
Most of these separate themes are implicit in or can be adduced
from the apocalyptic vision in Revelation 19:11–19, a compelling
depiction of the last days in which a mounted warrior, "clad with a
vesture dipped in blood," leads the "armies which were in heaven"
against "the beast and the kings of the earth"; in an image similar
to the messianic passage in Isaiah, "he treadeth the wine press of
the fierceness and wrath of Almighty God." Finally, he wears the
inscription, "King of kings, and Lord of lords." All these elements
of course look to the final eschatological fulfillment of the theological drama that the *Ordinalia* treats.

The ignorance of the angels at the approach of Christ is not
merely a dramatic technique, but was a traditional part both of
angelology and of the redemptive psychology. The nine orders of

angels represented in the nine angels who speak in the *Ordinalia* derive ultimately from the popular notions delineated by Dionysius the Pseudo-Areopagite, *On the Celestial Hierarchies* (ca. 500), and their questions are effectively similar to those ritually asked by the angels in the *Legenda aurea* of Jacobus de Voragine—who says he infers the questions from Dionysius.

The revelation of the resurrection thus proceeds from the Harrowing of Hell, where the infernal warriors ask, "pyv myghtern a lowene?" (who is the king of joy? *RD* 106), to the apparitions to the disciples—Mary Magdalene does not at first recognize Jesus and Thomas disbelieves her report to the last—and finally to the ascension, where the angels are at first bewildered. The redemption is therefore a "mystery" both sacramentally and psychologically. The doctrinal importance of this insistent theme requires separate treatment; for the moment, it is sufficient to observe its presence.

The ascension is, then, a kind of triumphal progress to the court of the King. The warrior who is at first marveled at but unrecognized by the seraphic courtiers is finally enthroned as the "king of heaven" (*RD* 2523, 2571, 2580), where he is at once the victorious warrior portrayed over the main portal of the medieval church and the *rex tremendae maiestatis* of the "Dies Irae," the figure of judgment invoked by the moving prayer for mercy in the liturgy for the dead. Into this conclusion the Cornish dramatist has woven his sources, whether biblical or legendary or symbolic, and with them he has gathered in the themes and impulses of his drama, drenched as they are in the doctrine and the traditions of the church.

4. *The* Ordinalia *and Doctrine*

THE INSTRUCTIONAL AIMS of the medieval drama, apparent as they are in its treatment of biblical history, may also be tested upon the claims and needs for theological edification of the laity. The history of Western thought in the Middle Ages is, after all, largely a record of intellectual activity within the Church, and the cerebral tournaments were, in the main, held at the court of the Queen of the Sciences. Even if, as unsophisticated and popular literature that appealed more to the eye and convivial spirits than to the mind of the beholder, the drama cannot be expected to contain depth or breadth or subtlety of theological ideas, nonetheless it was shaped by literate and able clerics who can be assumed to have had some familiarity with the ideological dimensions of the times. Therefore, a consideration of the notional tendencies in the drama against the background of important doctrinal issues in theological speculation can afford a deeper understanding both of the relationship of this popular theater to the sources of intellectual vitality and of the theological impulses in the drama itself.

When William Scawen reflected on doctrine in the Cornish *Ordinalia,* he concluded, with a rather genteel seventeenth century patriotic and Anglican indulgence, that "there is nothing in it savouring of the old bards or their poetry, nor having references to Merlyanisms, but a bare and sober relation of matter of fact . . . I cannot again but admire, that it is so unpolluted with the Arian or Pelagian heresies. There are, it is true, some inoffensive and harmless traditions, and a word may be let slip of the Virgin Mary; and in those traditions you may observe the concurrence of others." [1] If Scawen appears to have been straining the drama rather quaintly through his Anglican catechism, he nevertheless thought the work worthy of attention for the ideas and attitudes implicit in it. While I do not wish to pursue Scawen's own doctrinal hints, the exegetical focus of the drama suggests a doctrinal focus that does seem to me worthy of scrutiny. Since the *Ordinalia,* like the other cycles, concerns itself above all with the historical events that cumulatively assert the redemption of mankind, the theological doctrine or doctrines of redemption are critical parts of its structure.

The resurrection became, for biblical and Christian interpretation, the central event in human—and, indeed, in cosmic—history. The redemption of man is the central spiritual affirmation of the resurrection. Of the doctrinal problems raised by this theological implication of the Christian view of history, none, after the main lines of christology had been laid down in patristic thought, was perhaps more vital than that raised so eloquently by Gregory of Nyssa in the fourth century: Gregory asks rhetorically of God, "if he was as powerful as we have indicated, so that he could destroy death and gain entrance to life, why did he not do what he wanted to by a mere act of will? Why did he effect our salvation in a devious way, by being born and nurtured and by experiencing death in the process of saving man? He could have saved us without submitting to these things." [2] Given, that is, the omnipotence of God and the trinitarian identification or oneness of Christ with God, Gregory wonders why the elaborate scheme of the incarnation, human life, and passion of Christ should have been employed to bring about man's redemption, when the power to effect that redemption was otherwise available.

After dropping the schoolmasterish remark that "sick people do not prescribe to doctors their manner of treatment," Gregory goes on to formulate a rationale for the redemption that was to become doctrinally seminal in subsequent Christian thought. Granting that God is omnipotent, Gregory argues that the redemption should at the same time accord with all the other attributes of God —namely, his justice, goodness, and wisdom as well as his power. Since man's fall consisted in his yielding himself to the bondage of the devil, God's justice demanded that this contractual relationship between man and his enemy should be legitimately and not arbitrarily severed. God therefore contrived, by a kind of holy deceit that should repay in kind the deception first practiced on man in his state of innocence, that the devil himself should abrogate this contract. The devil, therefore, forfeits forever his claim to man by mistaking Christ, over whose divinity he of course exercised no power, for man, over whom he indeed did exercise power. "Hence it was that God, in order to make himself easily accessible to [the devil] . . . veiled himself in our nature. In that way, as it is with greedy fish, he might swallow the Godhead like a fishhook along with the flesh, which was the bait." [3]

Gregory's striking metaphor, crude though it may seem to a squeamish modern intellect, lodged itself securely in the imagination of his successors and, together with his argument, carried the day. Rufinus would later elaborate it, so that just as the fish who takes the bait "is itself dragged out of the deep to become a bait for other fish," so the devil, when he swallowed the bait of Jesus' body, "was immediately caught and, bursting the bars of the underworld, was dragged out from the abyss to become a bait for others." [4] St. Augustine himself would eventually and characteristically give his own fillip to the notion and make the metaphor his own by comparing the cross to a mousetrap baited for the devil with Christ's blood.[5]

The device for deception succeeded, at any rate, as Gregory argues, in manifesting all the attributes of God in the redemption: "That [God] decided to save us is proof of his goodness. That he struck a bargain to redeem the captive indicates his justice. And it is evidence of his transcendent wisdom that he contrived to make accessible to the enemy what was (otherwise) inaccessible . . .

His power is clear in this: that he came in the likeness of man and in the lowly form of our nature, inspiring the hope that, like man, he could be overcome by death; and yet, having come, he acted entirely in accordance with his nature." [6]

Gregory's fundamental rationale for the redemption, though it was elaborated and refined, nonetheless held securely for centuries; indeed it went almost unquestioned until it met so formidable an obstacle as St. Anselm at the end of the eleventh century. St. Anselm finished his brilliant treatise on the incarnation, *Cur Deus Homo,* in 1098. There he raised the objection that justice could be no issue between God and his infernal adversary: "For, though man deserved to be tormented by the devil, yet the devil tormented him unjustly. For man merited punishment, and there was no more suitable way for him to be punished than by that being to whom he had given his consent to sin. But the infliction of punishment was nothing meritorious in the devil . . . He did not do this at the command of God, but God's inconceivable wisdom, which happily controls even wickedness, permitted it." [7] For Anselm, consequently, it is from sinfulness, and not from the devil's power, that man has to be redeemed. Through his sin, man in the fall has infinitely affronted God; for that affront, an infinite "satisfaction" must be made; and since only God can offer such satisfaction, it is necessary that God become man in order to suffer voluntarily what man through the abuse of his own free will suffers necessarily—that is, death, which is the punishment entailed by sin. [8]

Anselm's argument, with its arresting and somewhat feudal view of the "honor of God," [9] in debasing which man's sin consists, has been generally known as the "satisfaction" theory—in contrast to the earlier "abuse of power" or "ransom" theory—of the redemption. Although this brief summary of Anselm's ideas can only be generally suggestive and is helpless to describe either the conceptual or the methodological genius of a work that represents the full and extraordinarily subtle ability of a splendid intellect, it will suffice to indicate something of the complexity that at this point entered the development of the doctrine. Anselm's argument did not, in fact, revolutionize the doctrine; it was not wholeheartedly accepted in the mainstream of thought nor did it generate a substantial controversy. It made its weight felt finally in Scholastic theology, but even then the method was probably more influential than the idea.[10] Its effects cannot be minimized, however, for it opened the way "for a fresh appreciation of the human sufferings of the Redeemer. The figure on the Cross was seen with a new clarity to be that of a Man. The Devil slipped out of the drama and left God and Man face to face." [11]

So far as the doctrine of the redemption figures in the drama— or, more specifically, in the *Ordinalia*—the most crucial point in its development probably belongs to the twelfth century. In 1140, just after the abortive council of Sens, St. Bernard of Clairvaux wrote to Pope Innocent II, "Here in France we have a new professor of theology, developed from an old doctor of dialectics, who, after having amused himself all his life with the logical art, is beginning now to make wild work with the Holy Scriptures." [12] The man upon whom St. Bernard's wrath fell was no less a personage than Peter Abelard. While all the reasons for this astonishing rupture, which found perhaps the two most imposing figures in the church of that day locked in a shattering doctrinal conflict, are difficult to trace or even clearly to arrange, something is known of the gathering storm which finally broke upon the bishops assembled in the king's presence at Sens during the octave of the feast of Pentecost, in 1140.[13]

In the previous year William of St. Thierry had written to both Bernard and the papal legate in France, Geoffrey the Bishop of Chartres, to warn them of and to demand the correction of heretical notions that he had found in Abelard's *Theologia*. Bernard may have met privately with Abelard to discuss their disagreements. Nonetheless, the Archbishop of Sens, at the instigation of Abelard's partisans, agreed to what Abelard seems to have anticipated would be a public dispute. It became, instead, probably under Bernard's influence, an ecclesiastical court prepared to judge the orthodoxy

of Abelard's ideas. Abelard avoided the confrontation by appealing
to the jurisdiction of Rome, whither Bernard's polemical epistle,
quoted above, made its way. In the event, Abelard was censured
and silenced, and his few remaining days were spent in autumnal
quiescence under the rule of Cluny.

When Bernard wrote the Pope, he chose to attack Abelard
at two vital points, on his view of the trinity and on the nature
of the redemption. Among the propositions in Abelard's work that
William of St. Thierry had pointed out as noxious to Bernard had
been the idea that "it was not in order to deliver us from the power
of the devil [that] Christ took flesh and suffered," [14] and here is
the germ of the idea that Bernard takes pains to refute in his letter
to the Pope.

Abelard's view of the redemption, the effect of which on the
traditional view was not unfairly described by William of St.
Thierry, can perhaps best be savored in its larger implications and
in the ethical context of what, for Abelard, sin and guilt were.
Simplified, Abelard's argument is based on his conviction that sin
is identifiable not merely with the contravention of God's will,
but rather with the contravention of what one knows to be God's
will. It is not sheer disobedience but willful and deliberate disobedience upon which Abelard fixes to explain the source of
human misery. The motive for the act rather than the act itself is
then the legitimate test of moral value. In applying this attitude,
for example, Abelard suggests what was generally unpalatable, that
the Jews did not sin in crucifying Jesus, because they were ignorant of what they did.[15]

By extending this view of sin, Abelard suggests that Adam's
posterity is not, in fact, guilty with him of the original sin of disobedience. Instead, all men are but bound by the penalty incurred
at Adam's sinning. The penalty is, indeed, to suffer at the hands
of the devil, yet (as Anslem also had argued) the devil has this
power over man not by right but by the sufferance of God: "His
itaque rationibus convinci videtur quod diabolus in hominem quem

seduxit nullum jus seducendo acquisierit, nisi forte, ut diximus, quantum ad permissionem Domini pertinebat, qui eum illi quasi carcerario vel tortori suo ad puniendum tradiderat." (These reasonings are seen to demonstrate that the devil, who led man astray, acquired no right in him thereby, unless, perhaps, as we have said, so much as the Lord permitted, who gave man over to the devil as his jailer or his torturer, for punishment.) [16]

The way to be free of this penalty is, rather than to endure the bondage of the devil, to embrace the service of God, which requires man to be obedient out of love, not out of fear. In order to manifest the love that leads to freedom from the penalty of sin, Christ was made flesh and endured the passion. The redemption is, consequently, a moral example, a persuasive paradigm of love:

Nobis autem videtur quod in hoc justificati sumus in sanguine Christi, et Deo reconciliati, quod per hanc singularem gratiam nobis exhibitam, quod Filius suus nostram susceperit naturam, et in ipsos nos tam verbo quam exemplo instituendo usque ad mortem perstitit, nos sibi amplius per amorem astrixit, ut tanto divinae gratiae accensi beneficio, nil jam tolerare ipsum vera reformidet charitas. Quod quidem beneficium antiquos Patres etiam hoc per fidem exspectantes, in summum amorem Dei tanquam homines temporis gratiae non dubitamus accendisse, cum scriptum sit: *Et qui praeibant et qui sequebantur clamabant dicentes Hosanna filio David,* etc. [Matthew 21:9]. Justior quoque, id est amplius Dominum diligens quisque fit post passionem Christi quam ante, quia amplius in amorem accendit completum beneficium quam speratum. Redemptio itaque nostra est illa summa in nobis per passionem Christi dilectio, quae non solum a servitute peccati liberat, sed veram nobis filiorum Dei libertatem acquirit, ut amore ejus potius quam timore cuncta impleamus, qui nobis tantam exhibuit gratiam qua major inveniri, ipso attestante, non potest. *Majorem hac,* inquit, *dilectionem nemo habet quam ut animam suam ponat pro amicis suis* [John 15:13].

(However, it seems to us that we are justified by the blood of Christ and reconciled to God, in this sense, that through this singular grace vouchsafed to us—that his son assumed our nature and, teaching us as much by word as by example, persevered even to death—he drew us closer to himself through love, so that once

we have been kindled by so great a gift of divine grace, true charity
does not fear to endure anything. We do not doubt that the self-
same gift kindled the highest love of God in the fathers of old, who
longed for it through faith, as it does in men who live in the time
of grace, since it is written, "And they that went before and they
that followed, cried, saying: Hosanna to the son of David, etc."
Moreover, he is more righteous, that is, he loves the Lord more
greatly, who is born after rather than before the passion of Christ,
for a favor enjoyed kindles greater love than a favor hoped for.
And so our redemption is that highest love which is ours thanks
to the passion of Christ, and which not only frees us from bondage
to sin, but acquires for us the true freedom of the sons of God,
so that we may be altogether filled with love rather than with fear
of him who conferred on us so much grace that, by his own testimony, none greater can be found. "Greater love than this," he
said, "no man hath, that a man lay down his life for his friends.") [17]

For Abelard, the battleground for the conflict between sin and
grace was rather psychological than cosmological. Just as sin proceeds from man's motives, so the redemption appeals to those motives.

To oppose this theological novelty, St. Bernard aims his fire
at two points in Abelard's argument. First, by minimizing the
claims of the devil, Abelard has threatened both to belittle the
enormity of sin and to cast doubt on the necessity of the redemption. Secondly, the view that Christ's suffering was redemptive
merely in affording man a kind of sublime example of love implies
that "all the glory of our redemption, all the merit of our salvation,
[lies] not in the virtue of the cross and Blood of Christ, but rather
in our own efforts after perfection." [18] Bernard sees clearly that
if, as Abelard suggests, "Christ has benefited us in no other way
than by giving us an example of virtue, with equal reason it can be
said that Adam has injured us in no other way than by giving us
an example of sin." [19] Bernard eloquently and fiercely rejects a
theology that he prefers scornfully to call a *stultologia,* and hurls

into the breach the traditional arguments about sin, the devil's power, and the nature of the redemption.

One cannot, however, simply take Bernard's letter for a conservative's vindication of tradition. Nor did this controversy fester into an intellectual crisis: Bernard's letter managed to silence Abelard, and the subject never again became fuel for such a fire. The significant implications and dimensions revealed in this dispute are, in fact, deeper and less obvious than a mere confrontation of these doctrinal positions can possibly indicate. Fundamental to this conflict, for example, is the essential antipathy between the rationalist and the mystic. Abelard sought above all to understand faith and to make it practicable. For Bernard, faith was essentially a matter of mystery. Behind Bernard's attack on Abelard lies his perception of the profound gulf fixed between the glory of God and the wretchedness of man: therefore, he complains that "this man by his fiction has rendered so plain and perspicuous to us [the 'mystery hidden from ages in God'] that it is now as a way through which everyone can easily pass, even the unclean and the uncircumcised!" [20]

When Abelard seeks to make a relationship between man and God more clear by building an epistemological bridge through human personality, the mystic rises to tear it down, at least partly because he seeks to establish such a relationship by effacing personality. Significantly, Bernard rests his appeal against Abelard finally in an ardent contemplation of the sacramental mystery of the eucharist: "To follow Jesus is a salutary purpose; to hold and embrace Him is joy inexpressible; but to eat His Flesh is blissful life . . . Therefore, neither the example of humility given us by Christ, nor the object-lesson of perfect charity, could avail us aught without the mystery of redemption." [21]

Such an appreciation for what amounts to an antipathy in their attitudes can afford an equally revealing view of the very considerable similarities in Abelard and Bernard. Despite the apparent juxtaposition of a new and a traditional view of the doctrine of redemption, both men share a prospect upon which earlier eyes had not looked. Indeed, their common differences with the past are no less significant, if more subtle, than the doctrinal views that divide them against one another.

Thus, when Bernard argues the necessity of redemption and justifies the means that God took to this end, he uses as the basis of his appeal neither Gregory of Nyssa's arguments from the properties of God nor Anselm's sense of the humanly unpayable obligation owed God from man. Instead, on the one hand he affirms that, at least in theory, God, being unconstrained, might have chosen any method to redeem man. On the other hand, he speculates that the incarnation and passion were perhaps chosen "for the reason that the sufferings of the Saviour, so great and so many, would bring and keep more strongly and vividly before our minds, in this 'land of oblivion,' the gravity of our fall." [22] Bernard is not simply making a concession to Abelard's view of the crucifixion, and he quickly draws back from his suggestion to assert that he only means to justify *how* and not *why* man has been redeemed. Nonetheless, this almost parenthetical remark, taken with the vivid language of sacrifice and his insistence on the mysterious efficacy of the spilled blood, reveals in its way how much more passionately and even intellectually than earlier apologists Bernard was aware of the human anguish and suffering manifested in the passion. Like Abelard, Bernard contemplates the figure on the cross with profound human sympathy, and the crucifixion is a distinctly human act even as it embodies the kernel of the mystery of divinity. In this sense both Abelard and Bernard were men of their times, and in this sense their argument has significance for the doctrinal import of subsequent literature.

Together with their awareness of the human feelings represented in the act of redemption, both Abelard and Bernard introduce into the doctrine an essential reliance on the love of God. God's love is central to both for explaining the redemption, and this insistence again helps to set off these two antagonists from

most earlier theorists.[23] To be sure, for Bernard this love is a
mystery at the very heart of things; for Abelard it is a kind of
ultimate justification in a rational scheme. Bernard would agree
with Abelard that in the suffering and death of Christ God's love
is revealed—but revealed sacramentally, he would caution, not
as an example; and possessing a soteriological efficacy of its own.
The two divide again, as mystic and rationalist would, since Bernard looks ecstatically on and longs to participate in the source
of love, while Abelard aims rather at an accessible dialectical defi-
nition of love: "the Abelardian doctrine of Divine love amounts
to this, that God is not to be loved as Abelard loved Heloise, but
as Heloise loved Abelard" [24]—not, in other words, for the sake of
one's own pleasure but for God's own sake. Yet despite their differences, both antagonists have made of the redemption a less
austerely cosmological and a more intensely human act than hitherto had been allowed.

St. Thomas Aquinas and his *Summa Theologica,* of course,
lies nearer in time to the medieval cycles than the two great con-
troversialists of the twelfth century. His discussion of the redemption, however, looks back in its intellectual premises to the earlier
builders upon the doctrine. He is, in method and in effect, syncretistic, and draws on Augustine as well as on Anselm. Indeed,
neither the spectacle of Christ's physical suffering nor the impulses
of divine love intrude, as in Abelard and Bernard, upon his
splendidly logical analysis of the redemption.

Aquinas treats first the causes and then the effects of man's
redemption.[25] He sees as the fundamental issue in redemption the
idea of the will—essentially, the will of God and its relation to the
will of Christ. God is not compelled to redeem man nor is Christ
compelled to suffer and to die. Yet God wills man's redemption
and Christ wills obedience to that will of God. If the ultimate justification for man's redemption is the will of God, the means for
effecting such redemption lies in the will of Christ. Therefore Christ
wills obedience to God, who wills man's deliverance: the conse-

quence of this mutual exercise of will is the incarnation, passion, and death of Christ. In such a scheme, the devil is without rights or power: man "did not become God's servant on account of his guilt, but rather, by withdrawing from God's service, he, by God's just permission, fell under the devil's servitude;" [26] and Aquinas is therefore able to distribute the effects of the redemption among the various earlier doctrines. Thus, Christ's passion "acts by way of satisfaction, inasmuch as we are liberated by it from the debt of punishment; while inasmuch as we are freed from the servitude of guilt, it acts by way of redemption; but in so far as we are reconciled with God it acts by way of sacrifice." [27] The implication of Aquinas' argument is to focus on Christ's passion essentially as a manifestation of obedience and as an ultimate test of the will.

This general summary of ideas can pretend to be neither an adequate historical survey nor a careful study of all representative types of thinkers who belong to the development of the idea of the redemption. The doctrine has been ably discussed and traced elsewhere.[28] Yet such a nexus of ideas is essential for attempting to locate the doctrinal subcurrents and implications in the drama. Indeed, it is necessary to hold in the hands some of the unraveled ends of threads that will be woven together into the very texture of later doctrinal attitudes.

In a stimulating essay on the doctrine of the redemption as it appears elsewhere in medieval drama, Timothy Fry has argued, in effect, that "the theory of the Redemption on which the *Ludus Coventriae* is built is known as the abuse-of-power theory in theological parlance, and was developed during the Patristic era." [29] He points out, for example, the inherent dramatic appeal of setting God and the devil as antagonists, and he has shown how this fundamental conflict ties together a number of incidents, from the seduction of Eve in the garden of Eden to the Harrowing of Hell, in forming a logical and persuasive ground for dramatic unity in the plays he discusses. Although Fry's study confines itself to the *Ludus Conventriae,* it raises important questions pertinent to all medieval drama, and the Cornish *Ordinalia* may itself profitably be set in such a general perspective.

The lineaments of the old and traditional view of the redemption as a kind of legal struggle for power over man between God and the devil are very evident and are fundamentally important in the *Ordinalia*. The first indication that the devil has acquired some power over man follows the murder of Abel, when the gloating devils carry off the dead man's soul to hell "that he may sing 'alas' ever in thick darkness" (*may hallo cane ellas/ nefre yn tewolgow tew: OM* 545–546). The drama does not make clear how this right or power was acquired, unless God's parting injunction to the devil in the garden be construed as an implicit justification: "and ever shall there be enmity," God explains, after Genesis 3:15, "between thy offspring and the offspring of woman":

> ha nefre y fyth avey
> yntre the lynneth the sy
> ha lynneth benen (*OM* 314–316).

The incident leaves uncertain the question of whether the devil is exercising a right or merely taking advantage of God's sufferance: that power over man has become the devil's prerogative is, at any rate, implicit in the scene.

More significant than the unresolved problem of the nature of diabolical authority is, perhaps, the early manifestation of ignorance on the devil's part. When Lucifer—who seems, in the heirarchy, to be foremost of the devils—has Abel brought to him forever "in thick darkness," he reveals his ignorance of God's prior assurance to Abel, which of course he did not hear, that because his "tithe is true, he shall find, in the end, unfailing joy ever, in my land and rest":

> rag bos abel gvyr thege
> ef a'n gefyth yn dyweth
> an ioy na thyfyk nefre
> yn ov gulas ha cosoleth (*OM* 515–518).

Thus early on, the crucial dramatic element of the "bargain" or "ransom" theory of the redemption takes hold firmly: the devil mistakes the terms of the arrangements. He is aware of God's wrath toward man, but he is ignorant of the promised redemption.

The dramatic significance of this ignorance is reinforced at the death of Adam. Once again, the devils come to carry off the dead, gleefully anticipating the eternity of misery in which they will be able to torture him. Immediately before his death, however, Adam has received through Seth the reassurance, first mentioned at the expulsion from the garden (*OM* 328–330), that God will vouchsafe the "oil of mercy" to himself and his progeny in alleviation of the consequences of his first sin. The angel had, after all, informed Seth about the new-born babe seen amid the upper branches of the tree in paradise:

> Mab dev o neb a wylsys
> avel flogh byhan maylys
>   ef a bren adam the das
> gans y gyk ha wos kefrys
> pan vo termyn denythys
>   ha'th vam hag ol an dus vas
> ef yv an oyl a versy
>   a fue the'th tas dythywys
> dre y vernans yredy
>   ol an bys a fyth sylwys.

(The Son of God it was whom thou sawest, like a little child swathed. He will redeem Adam, thy father, with his flesh and blood, too, when the time is come; and thy mother, and all the good people. He is the oil of mercy, which was promised to thy father; through his death, clearly, all the world will be saved: *OM* 809–818.)

The doctrinal irony of Lucifer's misunderstanding is quickly apparent when, directly Adam is dead, Lucifer, calling him a "good purchase" (*vn purvers da: OM* 882), claims him, and the lesser devils insist that "now he is our fellow" (*lemyn ef yv agan guas: OM* 910), and that he will endure an everlasting punishment (*OM* 888–889, 897–898, 903–904). Already, then, the drama has prepared for the fundamental conflict that flares again at the beginning of the *Passio Christi* and becomes finally a kind of climactic issue in the last day's play with the Harrowing of Hell. The devil fails to perceive the limitations that God has fixed on his power over man. In the incarnation and death of Jesus those limitations will be asserted as God's will prevails over the devil's ignorance through the kind of "holy deceit" stipulated in patristic thought about the redemption.

The drama begins on the second day with an appropriate recollection of this conflict that has been so firmly established. The first incident in the *Passio Christi* is the temptation of Christ. The temptation serves not only to establish the fact of the incarnation—thereby, incidentally, making the doctrinal point that would eventually be made in other cycles by the nativity plays—but also to emphasize its significance for the redemption, within the terms of the cosmic conflict already prepared.

The scene opens with Jesus warning his disciples about the wiles of the devil:

> yowynk ha lovs · kyn fo tollys
> dre y deunos · mercy gylwys
> scon y gallos · a vyth lehys
> mercy yw stos · the nep a'n pys.

(Young and grey, though you be deceived by his subtilty, call for mercy; soon his power shall be lessened. Mercy is extended to whoever prays for it: *PC* 19–22.) The idea recurs as Jesus prepares for his ordeal at the devil's hands:

> penys a reys · ragh y terros
> may fo leheys · mvr a y gallos
> dre ow fynys.

(Penance is necessary, that his arrogance may be diminished, the greatness of his power, by my pains: *PC* 43–45.)

Satan at once states that he intends to tempt Christ in order to determine whether or not he is a god (*PC* 48–49), and after the three temptations, which are set down simply and without elaboration of the biblical narrative, he concludes:

go vy vyth pan yth thotho
pan of fythys thyworto
    ter-gwyth hythew
ha'n maystri bras ol a'm bo
my re'n collas quyt dretho
    may canaf trew.

(Woe is me, that I went to him, that I am vanquished by him
three times today; and all the great power which was mine, I have
lost it quite through him, that I may sing 'alas!': *PC* 145–150.) Indeed, this encounter seems virtually to settle the question of the
devil's power since, in his failure to repeat with Jesus the success
that he enjoyed in his seduction of Eve, the devil would appear to
have disencumbered himself of his illusions about the extent of his
authority.

The matter does not end there, however. The dream of Pilate's
wife becomes another occasion for treating the issue of Satan's
power. In view of what has happened during the temptations of
Jesus, it is surprising suddenly to find here the devils confessing
that they have hitherto been deceived and have only just discovered
that Jesus is indeed the son of God.[30] Lucifer expresses a fear that
Jesus will diminish the power of the devils, and Satan concurs, in-
sisting that hitherto he had not been known to be the son of God.
In order to forestall the consequences of Christ's murder, about
which all the devils are apprehensive, Beelzebub is dispatched to
warn Pilate's wife so that, like Shakespeare's Calpurnia, she may
employ her uxorial wiles to avert the threatening disaster. An old
apocryphal legend is thus employed to reaffirm the traditional struggle of the devil to retain his accustomed power.

The themes emerge again finally and most clearly in the episode that both dramatically and doctrinally most closely conforms
to the old patristic doctrine of the redemption. In the Harrowing
of Hell the devils collectively fail to recognize Christ or his authority, and the scene comprises a bloodless but decisive encounter
of power. The lordly Lucifer anticipates a visit from the dead Jesus
when he holds a council of war and confesses,

ogh my re bue boghes coynt
hagh eth yn rak re a poynt
pur wyr pan wruk the pylat
lathe cryst rag ef gans cam
a gergth thyworthy'n adam.

(Oh, I have been little cunning, and went forward too much point-blank, truly, when I made Pilate kill Christ; for he with wrong will fetch Adam from us: *PC* 3031–3035.)

The dramatic encounter between the Spirit of Christ and Lucifer is simple and brief. The dramatist fixes typically on the rhetorical exchange in Psalms 24:7–10, yet when the devils ask, "Who is the king of glory?" they do so not rhetorically but in bewilderment. Thus their ignorance is again manifest, and as the gates fall before a triumphant redeemer, the issue of power over man is easily and quickly settled. After the deliverance from hell, Adam explains the whole drama, as it were, to Enoch, whom he meets as one of the blessed who have hitherto escaped the pains of hell in paradise:

gerhemmyn dev a terrys
dre henna y fuf dampnys
    the vos neffre yn yfern
ow arluth cryst dr'y vercy
a wruk ow dysprenne vy
mes a yfarn yn teffry
    gans y kyc ha'y wos keffrys
an enefow a ponow
y's dros omma the'n golow.

(I broke the command of God; through that I was condemned to be ever in hell. My Lord Christ, by his mercy, did redeem me out of hell, really, with his flesh and blood also. The souls from pains he brought here to the light: *RD* 212–220.)

Again at the ascension Christ is represented as a warrior and his struggle is described in military terms that emphasize a contention between powers. The angels, who, like the devils before them, are ignorant of Christ's identity, are told of the crucifixion in an extensive military metaphor that recalls the episode of the Harrowing of Hell:

> myghtern of a lowene
> ha'n victory eth gyne
> yn arvow ruth.

(I am the king of joy, and the victory goes with me, in red arms: *RD* 2520–2522.)

In all these scenes, an underlying sense of a divine struggle for power against the devil recalls the traditional patristic view of the redemption. Important differences remain, however. Most obviously, the drama avoids the implication of this view, so forcibly present, for example, in the "fishhook" and "mousetrap" metaphors, that God deceived the devil into mistaking Christ for any other man. The devils are deceived, to be sure, but the drama is at pains to emphasize that this deception is self-practiced and maintained in spite of abundant evidence to the contrary. Both in carrying off Abel and Adam to an eternal punishment despite the prior assurances given by God and in failing to recognize Christ as divine after the temptations, the devils deceive themselves both about the extent and about the validity of their power over man.

In a second though related departure from the old view, the drama evades the affirmation that the devil has acquired certain rights over man. Bernard himself had not defended the idea of the devil's rights. He preferred to emphasize the power of the devil, since the imputation of any rights over man to the devil increasingly seemed an embarrassing aspersion on the justice or goodness of God. In the *Ordinalia,* too, the struggle with Lucifer is not nearly so legally conceived, on the basis of the attributes of God, as it is pitched upon the sheer issue of power.[31] The drama, in brief, looks at the traditional view of the redemption as if through St. Bernard's eyes.

Still, this discussion of the *Ordinalia*'s affinities for the traditional doctrine only partially reconstructs its dramatic approach to the matter, which is far more complex than a sheer struggle between cosmic powers would allow. A consideration of episodes and themes less customarily associated with the patristic tradition makes clear the breadth and depth of this complexity.

A principal modification of the traditional view is apparent in the drama's concern with questioning the necessity for this particular scheme of redemption. If the Harrowing of Hell at the beginning and the ascension at the end of the *Resurrexio Domini* implicitly affirm a doctrine based on the conflict of power, of no less significance are the intervening scenes of the apostle Thomas' doubt, which deal with this very question of necessity.

In what may be the most intensely dramatic episode in the *Ordinalia,* Thomas receives Mary Magdalene's report of Jesus' resurrection with bitter disbelief. He rails against the girl's credibility and against the other apostles' credulity. Not because he is disillusioned or cynical but because he is above all a rationalist, Thomas mounts an impressive case against the likelihood of the resurrection. His arguments bear rehearsing in some detail. Thomas first points out that "never on any account can anyone be risen again after dying":

> byth ny yl awos an bys
> den vyth bones dasserhys
> wose merwel (*RD* 938–940).

When James the Greater insists that God's will alone is sufficient to overcome the impediment of such merely physical laws, Thomas reiterates that "a man who is dead, certainly will live again no more" (*den a vo marow certan / ny thasvew nes: RD* 948–949). John again emphatically defends the seeming credulity of the other disciples, and yet again Thomas points out what he knows: "Christ through suffering was quite done to death on the cross" (*cryst a fue dre galarow / yn grous pren gurys pur varow: RD* 962–963).

Bartholomew then makes the crucial point, one that Jesus had earlier insisted upon to Peter when the apostle had rushed to pre-

vent his master's capture (*PC* 1161–1170), that "no man would
have had power to put him to death. He was willing to die":

> ny'n gyfye den gallos
> > the'n mernens y worre ef
> ragon y fynnes merwel (*RD* 966–968).

This argument recalls Anselm's conviction that the efficacy of
Christ's satisfaction depended on his willing submission to the will
of God. Thomas grieves for his memory of the excruciating spectacle of Christ's suffering, and cogently replies that if God had the
power to effect man's salvation, he must also have been able to
effect it in another fashion, without suffering the agony of death:
"without dying, God could cause every man to be saved" (*dev a
alse hep merwel / gul the pup den ol sylwel: RD* 974–975). This
point, it will be remembered, had bothered theologians long before
Thomas used it here. The problem underlies the whole argument
of Gregory of Nyssa, who seeks above all to explain why God
chose this particular means to the redemption, and it glimmers
briefly in Bernard's letter to the Pope when he permits himself a
moment of speculation. The *Ordinalia,* however, does not follow
either Gregory's response, based on the nature of God, or Bernard's
tentative proposal—that of all the methods available to him, perhaps God chose the ignominy of suffering and death on the cross
in order most effectively to impress upon man the profoundest
significance of his redemption. Instead, Matthew smothers the debate with his caustic suggestion that God might, indeed, have taken
an easier way—he might simply have obliterated all creation, and
saved himself a great deal of trouble (*RD* 977–979).[32]

During the rest of the colloquy, Mary Magdalene elaborates
what she has seen, the apostles declare their belief, and Thomas
persists in his disbelief while clarifying his motives:

> a ty iacob bew a pe
> y seruont me a vye
> > fest yn lowen
> sav ef ny vew gas the son

> an dreyn bys yn ympynnyon
> eth yn y pen.

(Ah, thou James, if He were alive, His servant I would be right
gladly; but he is not alive—quit thy noise!—the thorns went into
his head even to the brains: *RD* 1007–1012.) The disturbing
problem that Thomas has raised by basing his conviction of the
implausibility of a resurrection on the incongruity, uselessness, and
needlessness of such a method on the part of one powerful enough
to achieve his ends at less cost to himself is not laid to rest in this
exchange with the disciples.

The question continues to vex the drama, since in the following episode the two disciples on their way to Emmaus make the
same point. Having heard a rumor of the resurrection, they prepare to return in order to verify it, but one of the two observes
that "on no account was it necessary to go so far as to put to death
the son of God of heaven":

> awos trauyth nynso reys
> mos the worre the'n mernes
> map dev a'n nef (*RD* 1252–1254).

When Jesus himself joins them, though unrecognized, he immediately remarks that "it was necessary for Christ to go into the
tomb" (*reys o the cryst mos yn beth: RD* 1276): the confutation
stands, of course, but without explanation.

Curiously enough, the problem is never really set to rest in
the *Ordinalia*. Although Jesus visits the other apostles in Thomas'
absence, Thomas on his return continues in his disbelief: he insists
that they are either deluded or lying. And when the two disciples
return from Emmaus with word of their experiences, he makes
what was probably a properly skeptical contemporary slur on the
veracity of the threadbare pilgrims always to be met with and
marveled at upon the medieval highways.[33] When at last Jesus does
return dramatically to encounter the doubting apostle, the issue
does not arise. The sight of his Lord persuades Thomas that Christ
has indeed risen from the dead and that his passion has "painfully

redeemed the Christians" (*yn tyn . . . the prenne / an grys-tonnyon: RD* 1543–1544). The troubled apostle no longer doubts or considers that his Lord's passion may not have been necessary.

It seems appropriate to note that if the deceitfulness of God was an embarrassing problem in the "ransom" theory of the redemption, not less problematical in Anselm's argument was the implication that man had necessarily to be redeemed in just such a way in order to satisfy the outraged "honor of God." The *Ordinalia* is obviously troubled by both problems, and it deals decisively with neither. The problem of necessity is important in *Cur Deus Homo,* for Anselm begins with the mutually exclusive alternatives—that man either can or cannot be saved. Given God's power it follows that man can be saved, and given God's goodness ("lest it should seem that God had repented of his good intent, or was unable to accomplish his designs"—I, xxv), man has necessarily to be saved. Anselm denies that the necessity for saving man lays any constraint on God, since he insists that for God thus to behave as God involves neither compulsion nor restraint (II, v, xviii). Once Anselm had argued for the redemption by appeal to necessity, however, the notion of necessity continued to trouble thinkers and theologians. The *Ordinalia* manifests the same persistent theological disquietude on the subject that characterized the work of most subsequent thinkers, but as might be expected, it does not attempt a theological solution to the problem: first the disciples and then Jesus affirm that "it was necessary," and there is an end to questions.[34]

Throughout the play the problem of Jesus' identity is troublesome. Not only do the angels at the ascension and the devils at the Harrowing of Hell fail to recognize in Jesus the incarnation of divinity, but this very recognition becomes an absorbing theme, sometimes as a kind of test of faith, throughout the drama. The incident of Maximilla's martyrdom in the *Origo Mundi,* based as it is on her invocation of a Christ not yet born, anticipates the epistemological tension that becomes central in the *Passio Christi.* The characters are divided most significantly on the question of whether Jesus is indeed the son of God. Though the principal reason for Jesus' condemnation (along with the insinuation that he is seditious) is the rejection of his claim to the divine patrimony,[35] a veritable parade of the faithful repeatedly asserts that claim. The songs and brief exclamations of the *pueri hebreorum,* the restored cripples, Mary Magdalene, Longinus after his healing, and a centurion in the concluding episode of the crucifixion repeatedly affirm that Jesus is indeed the son of God.[36]

This interest is epitomized in an episode that appears to be a mild and possibly unintended parody of a scholastic dispute. At Jesus' trial two learned doctors are sent for in order to dispute against Jesus (*PC* 1625–1628). They both promptly and confidently agree to come along in order to confute Jesus' claim to be the son of God (*PC* 1653–1664), but when at last they have an opportunity to try their dialectical skills against him, Jesus frustrates their resolution by refusing to utter a word in his own behalf. The learned disputants are not confounded, however, for they promptly set about formally arguing with one another. At the heart of their argument, which is, oddly, staged twice (*PC* 1729–1768, 2383–2476), lies the question of the two natures: whether, that is, both godhood and manhood can reside in the flesh together. The second doctor stipulates that such a notion is heresy and that Jesus himself is a charlatan. His venerable colleague, however, points out that the mermaid is a well-known example of the union of two natures in one being (*PC* 1739–1744, 2403–2404) and therefore that Jesus is not so quickly or easily to be dispatched. Although at the conclusion of their first dispute the first doctor agrees with seeming approval that Jesus is to come to an "evil end" (*drok dywethe: PC* 1828), the second dispute ends with the two doctors in hearty disagreement. The first doctor affirms that "he is the son of God of heaven" (*rag ef yv map dev a nef: PC* 2461), and the second archly remarks that "it is better that he die, than that the people be lost and condemned to darkness":

> guel yv y vos ef marow
> ys bos an popel kellys
> ha dampnys the tewolgow (*PC* 2464–2466)

—an ironic remark that may be based dramatically on the reiterated fear that Jesus has threatened to tear down the temple.[37]

The first doctor's curious use by analogy of the mermaid (*morvoren*) to explain rationally the rather problematical concept known as the "hypostatic union" is an unusual if not unique example of its kind.[38] The significance of the episode lies mainly in its use of what purports to be a cerebral debate between two recognizable types of learned men in order to buttress a principal theme of the drama. The first of the two doctors persuades himself that Jesus can be and in fact is the son of God. Since the question of recognition of Jesus' divinity is everywhere evident in the *Ordinalia,* this incident may be an effort on the part of the dramatist to elaborate his theme. Since, too, the *Ordinalia* rarely, and then usually for significant thematic reasons, as in the case of the legend of the cross, departs from a fairly basic fidelity to biblical or biblical-legendary history, this interpolation of a debate is doubly important.

Although the exchange between the doctors cannot but be regarded as a stand-off forensically, the supposedly rational fashion in which the first doctor reaches the conclusion that Jesus is indeed divine anchors the doctrine of the incarnation in reason as well as in mystical experience. If the various miracles—the rescue of the burning prophetess, the healing of the lame, the restoration of sight to the blind Longinus—persuade mystically, if the Harrowing of Hell and the ascension persuade cosmologically, then this debate seems intended to persuade rationally that the incarnation is a fact of faith.

This persistent concern for revealing the identity of Christ, based as it is on the significance of the doctrine of the incarnation, lies behind another important aspect of the attitude in the *Ordinalia* toward the redemption. The *Ordinalia* lays great stress on the crucifixion as a manifestation of Jesus' obedience, almost as a test of his will. The thrice-uttered prayer before the betrayal is thus exploited dramatically. "Remove this cup from me; yet not what I will, but what thou wilt" (Mark 14:36; cf. Matthew 26:39, 42, Luke 22:42): in the *Ordinalia* this reiterated prayer is subtly expanded, given prominence, and varied so that on the third occasion the point becomes especially clear.

> (1) gorre an keth mernans-ma
> thyworthyf na vyf lethys
> lemyn na fo ol ow bouth
> cowlynwys thy'mmo lemyn
> sav the voth the gy arluth
> bethens gruys yn pup termyn.

(Put away this same death from me, that I be not slain; but let not my will be fulfilled now, but let thy will, Lord, be done always: *PC* 1035–1040.)

> (2) ow tas ma ny yl bones
> may treylyo mernens the ves
> sav y wothaf thy'm a reys
> the volnegeth re bo gures
> rak an scryptor bynyges
> reys yv y vos guyr porrys.

(My father, if death cannot be turned away, but I must suffer it, [then] let thy will be done, for the blessed Scripture must needs be true: *PC* 1069–1074.)

> (3) mar syv the voth grant an spas
> na theffo thy'm an mernans
> sav ma ny yl bos nahen
> the voth prest yn pup hehen
> y goulenwel yv ow whans.

(If it be thy will, grant the while that death may not come to me; but if it cannot be otherwise, my wish is always in everything to fulfill thy will: *PC* 1088–1092.)

The emphasis is Anselm's, though, in one sense or another, Bernard and Abelard, Aquinas and Bonaventure would agree: Jesus did not will his own death, but he did will, above all, to be obedient to God's will. God's will is that men shall be saved—the promise of the oil of mercy, so important and so often invoked in the drama, assures it—and salvation must of necessity involve Jesus' death. The insistence on necessity as a rationale for the crucifixion has already been noted, and it can thus be seen to be of a piece with the idea that the psychology is at least as essential as the cosmology of redemption.[39]

When Peter strikes off Malchus' ear as Jesus is seized, Jesus reminds Peter of the necessity of his suffering (*PC* 1167–1170); on the other hand, when Mary his mother weeps over the shame and suffering of his death, the apostle John reminds her that Jesus suffers not helplessly but of his own will (*PC* 2952–2954), and immediately after the resurrection Jesus himself appears to assure her that he is well and that his passion is felicitously fulfilled with the promise of everlasting life and victory over death and pain (*RD* 423–510).

As the medieval cycles grew in length and added episodes, the representation of the crucifixion itself became longer and more gruesomely pictorial in detail. Fry has suggested that this obvious and growing preoccupation with the horrors of Jesus' suffering indicates a proportionate shift in medieval interest away from the traditional theological implications of the redemption to a more contemplative awareness of suffering itself. Certainly medieval art and thought dwelt increasingly on the human anguish of Jesus: eventually the rapturous author of *A Talking of the Love of God* could view the crucifixion in astonishingly and essentially sensual terms,[40] and the crucifixion portrayed on the Isenheim altar by Matthias Grünewald (ca. 1516) would depict the suffering of Jesus with a kind of grotesque and Gothic realism that, with its absorption in the painful details of Jesus' torment, almost blots out the doctrinal questions about the nature of the redemption.[41]

The seeds of such an interest are, of course, obvious in Abelard's view of the paradigmatic value of Christ's passion. Yet the emphasis is not on a rational but on a sympathetic apprehension of the significance of the event. The more luridly representational the scene of the crucifixion, the more it would appeal to the beholder's emotions and the less it could sustain the doctrinal emphases on the redemption as an act of God. For at least one writer, the mystery plays "formed an important element in that devotion to the Person and Passion of Christ which was so characteristic" of the fourteenth century.[42]

None of the medieval cycles shunts the crucifixion offstage: it is, after all, the climax of the biblical drama. Indeed, all the cycles indulge the more or less bloodthirsty and bloodcurdling possibilities inherent in the representation of an execution. Yet some of the plays allow the mordant business a disproportionate amount of time. A modern audience would probably not be particularly fascinated by the relish of the executioners as they batter the thorns into Jesus' skull or delightedly wrench his arms out of their sockets to reach the nail holes carelessly bored too far apart in the cross beam —not so fascinated, at any rate, as to wish that the torture should be prolonged. Yet such violence can add to the appeal of a spectacle, if not to the coherence of a drama. The pleasure taken by the medieval drama in dwelling on such scenes may, then, owe more of its enthusiasm to the taste of the gallery than to the theological preoccupations of the playwright, although violence as a theme does not manifestly impair doctrinal concern. For present purposes, I only note that several such scenes occur in the Ordinalia; this drama, too, is aware that it must first delight its spectators if it wishes to teach them.

On balance, then, the Ordinalia is doctrinally more muddled than clear in its treatment of the redemption. Fry has suggested that the Ludus Coventriae has both a dramatic and a doctrinal unity based on a predominantly patristic affinity for the "abuse of power" theory of the redemption.[43] If the same judgment were to be made about the *Ordinalia,* no such sweeping affirmation could apply. There is, as I have tried to show, a great deal in the drama to suggest that what basically is at issue is a struggle between God and the devil for sovereign rights over man. Nonetheless this fundamental cosmological struggle loses much if not nearly all its force in such alien concerns as Thomas' effectively dramatic suspicion that the crucifixion was not necessary; or in the psychological and human appeal that the sheer spectacle of the trial, torture, and crucifixion has over the broader issue.

Furthermore, a great deal of the ideological justification for the traditional theory of the atonement lay in the idea that God overcame the devil not by power but by a just and legal device that involved a holy deceit, dependent on the devil's failure or inability to recognize the divinity hidden in Christ's humanity. Although the drama seems generally to keep the theme of the devil's ignorance on this point, at the same time it makes a recognition of Jesus' identity crucial, plausible, and vital on the part of the men he is sent to redeem. By way of summary, it seems fair to say that the *Ordinalia* manifests a deep awareness of the various ideas that had made the doctrine of the redemption something of a lively issue in its time, and takes most of them into account. Equally striking, however, is its unwillingness or inability to reconcile them.

Such a statement does not intend to imply that the drama applied a thin varnish to a doctrine that was falling to pieces. The cycles would surely never have been so popular had they sought to resolve issues that went to the heart of changes or disputes in theological methods and attitudes, particularly since those doctrinal struggles were carried on within a large and complex system that rested on the assumption of ecclesiastical unity. Indeed the business of the biblical cycles was more probably to insist on doctrinal unity than to stimulate speculation amongst the laity on matters that might be divisive. The failure of the *Ordinalia* to present a systematic doctrinal explanation of the redemption upon which it focuses is, then, indicative less of intellectual ignorance or ineptitude in the dramatist than of a failure of consensus in the times. The dramatist is at least implicitly aware of most of the chief questions that had been raised against the earliest interpretations of the doctrine of the redemption and is no more willing than Aquinas satisfactorily to meet all objections, no more able than Bernard to pronounce for a single, unified, and coherent explanation.

Such a conclusion requires some important qualifications. Chiefly it must be urged that this essay deals only with a single doctrinal issue, and views the *Ordinalia* against the thought and writings that lie behind that doctrine only. Scholars are increasingly aware of the astonishing amount of what we should regard today as controversy that flourished in a medieval period often carelessly regarded as intellectually monolithic. These observations on one doctrinal matter—albeit an important one—are not therefore intended as generalizations that will hold for all.

Furthermore, the drama was not alone among medieval works that undertook to edify the laity, and the problem of doctrinal underpinnings emerges elsewhere. A fascinating and parenthetically pertinent case in point is *Piers Plowman*. The great fourteenth century poem is itself something of a conundrum on the doctrine of redemption. For example, Greta Hort argues that the poet is basically in harmony with St. Anselm in his view of the atonement, since "the root-ideas are in both cases a debt due from man to God, on the payment of which the reconciliation of God's mercy and justice depends. It is a debt which man cannot pay, but which Christ has paid for him by freely giving his life to God." [44]

Robert Worth Frank, on the other hand, distinguishes and discusses three different emphases in the poem on Christ's role in the redemption.[45] Though the poem may be seen broadly as an exceptional example of the popular imitation-of-Christ literature, with its exemplaristic implications for the redemption, Hort's emphasis on the Anselmian idea can equally be seen, particularly in the life of Dobet. Yet in the vision of B. Passus XVIII, basically a narrative of the crucifixion and Harrowing of Hell, the familiar old patristic emphasis on the ransom is predominant. The poem wavers, however, even in dealing with this motif. When the dreamer asks Faith whether Piers is at the tournament in Jerusalem, his catechist replies, continuing the metaphor,

> This Iesus of his gentrice · wole Iuste in Piers armes,
> In his helme and in his haberioun · *humana natura;*
> That Cryst be nouȝt biknowe here · for *consummatus deus*
>   (B. XVIII, 22–24).[46]

C.XXI, 20 adds the "free will of God" (*liberum-dei-arbitrium*) as the instigator of the "joust," thereby injecting a note from Anselm, but the knightly disguise is fundamentally a chivalric version of the familiar metaphors of the holy deceit.

As in the Cornish *Ordinalia,* the devils discuss their strategy immediately before Jesus' invasion of hell, but in *Piers Plowman* they conduct an argument about their rights to or claim on man (B. XVIII, 263–303) which reads like a discussion of the controversial writing that had dealt with this particular matter. When Jesus himself justifies his action, he first insists that "bi riȝt and by resoun" he has come to "ranceoun here my lyges" (B. XVIII, 347). He goes on to insist that he undoes by grace what Lucifer had done by guile, but the language of the old legal maneuver prevails when Jesus asserts the validity of his using "guile against guile":

> And as Adam and alle · thorw a tre deyden,
> Adam and alle thorwe a tree · shal torne aȝeine to lyue;
> And gyle is bigyled · and in his gyle fallen:
>   *Et cecedit in foueam quam fecit* (355–358).[47]

The C version, interestingly enough, omits this frank reiteration of the theme of holy deceit. At any rate, *Piers Plowman* has its own troubles with the idea. When set alongside the later and much greater English poem, it is not for exhibiting more doctrinal confusion that the Cornish drama appears as the lesser literary sun.

Finally, study of the contemporary doctrinal climate ought to inform our critical reading of all the instructional literature with which the *Ordinalia* belongs. Not until most of the rest of the medieval biblical drama is viewed in the same context can any of it appear adequately in perspective.[48] Only when we better understand the relationship of the drama to the intellectual and doctrinal concerns of its time—however changing such a relationship may prove to be—can these conclusions properly be tested.

The immediate aim is a modest one, then, and seeks chiefly to illuminate the Cornish *Ordinalia*. If this study has emphasized the contradictions and uncertainties in the plays, it is no less aware of the relative doctrinal sophistication of a dramatist who, after all, only reflects the unsettled ideas of his theological heritage.

5. The Ordinalia *and the Liturgy*

THE STORY OF THE drama's growth out of the proliferating ceremonies of the Western Church is, thanks to the significant labors of Karl Young and others, well known and well established. The seeds of drama were always in the rite of the Mass, which itself was generally recognized among medieval liturgiologists to be a kind of re-enactment of man's salvation through the passion and death of Christ.[1] The best known and most influential of the medieval commentators was William Durandus, Bishop of Mende (ca. 1230–1296), in whose compendious *Rationale divinorum officiorum* it may truly be said that "the Mass is understood as a dramatic presentation of an action in the divine economy, especially of the suffering, death and resurrection of Christ, beginning with the longings and sighs of the patriarchs and prophets and concluding with our Saviour's ascension into heaven." [2] Indeed, Durandus himself remarked that "Missae officium tam provida reperitur ordinatione dispositum, ut quae per Christum et in Christum, ex quo de coelo descendit, usque dum in coelum ascendit, gesta sunt, magna ex parte contineat, et ea tam verbis, quam signis admirabili quadam specie repraesentet." (The ceremony of the Mass is found to be ordered in such provident fashion that it contains in great part those things done by Christ and in Christ from the time that he came down from heaven until he ascended into heaven, and it portrays them, in a certain marvelous fashion, as much by words as by signs.) [3]

Gradually, the church began to make use of and to elaborate

this dramatic element. The various dramatic compositions that found their places in the services of worship bear witness to the ease and popularity with which the efforts at overt dramatization were welcomed and absorbed into the ritual of the church.[4] The fully developed vernacular cycles, of which the *Ordinalia* is the Cornish species, are closely related and heavily indebted to the earlier drama which belonged to the altar and presbyters rather than to the marketplace and the laity. Most of the episodes correspond, although in the cycles they are joined together and elaborated and sometimes significantly altered.

The conjunction of various episodes, all of which have their roots more or less securely in the liturgical practices of the church, did not result in organizational chaos. Since the dramatic representations that had grown up in the liturgy were essentially historical, aimed at reproducing the biblical events that lay behind and explained the ritual events, the biblical cycles had a coherent plan ready for the using. In fact, if the Mass was itself a handy compendium of scriptural history, the liturgical year was similarly organized about a scheme of readings, festivals, and seasons that recall fairly exactly the biblical history of man's redemption. By tracing the Old Testament plays in the various vernacular cycles to the pre-Lenten and Lenten emphases in the church year rather than to the *Processus Prophetarum* alone,[5] Craig and Kretzmann were able to associate the sequence of the plays in the dramatic cycles with the structure of the church year itself.[6]

Against this background, establishing a general relationship between liturgical practices and the drama, we may profitably inquire more closely into the *Ordinalia* for various reflections or manifestations of such a relationship. The inquiry, of course, again seeks to elucidate the instructional aims of the drama. The search begins naturally enough in an examination of the variety, frequency, and nature of overt liturgical allusions to be found in the plays.

The very name by which the Cornish cycle is known points to

the liturgy. The term *ordinalia* is taken from the introductory headings prefixed to the first and third day's play, each of which begins "hic incipit Ordinale." Du Cange cites Linwodus' gloss of the *ordinale* as "liber in quo ordinatur modus dicendi et solemnizandi divinum officium" (a book that prescribes the manner of saying and celebrating the divine office).[7] The *ordinale* or ordinal, then, was "essentially a Service Book for choir use. From one point of view it may be said to contain the application in detail of the general liturgical and ceremonial principles laid down in the Consuctudinary. From another point of view it may be called a guide book to the rest of the Service Books." [8] As Frere notes, it was the book upon which depended the proper execution of a community's services of worship. Since it functioned as a kind of stage manager's guide to the rites and ceremonies of the church, the appropriation of its name to describe the written text of the drama is understandable.

The term "ordinary," used to describe the prompter in Richard Carew's amusing anecdote, is somewhat analogous, and its usage was widespread. Carew observed in 1602 that in presenting the plays,

the players con not their parts without book, but are prompted by one called the ordinary, who followeth at their back with the book in his hand, and telleth them softly what they must pronounce aloud. Which manner once gave occasion to a pleasant conceited gentleman of practising a merry prank; for he undertaking (perhaps of set purpose) an actor's room, was accordingly lessoned (beforehand) by the ordinary, that he must say after him. His turn came: quoth the ordinary, 'Go forth man, and show thyself.' The gentleman steps out upon the stage, and like a bad clerk in scripture matters, cleaving more to the letter than the sense, pronounced these words aloud. 'Oh (says the fellow softly in his ear) you mar all the play.' And with this his passion the actor makes the audience in like sort acquainted. Hereon the prompter falls to flat railing and cursing in the bitterest terms he could devise; which the gentleman with a set gesture and countenance still soberly related, until the ordinary, driven at last into mad rage, was fain to give over all.[9]

The text of Bodl. MS. 791, or the text of which it is a copy, was probably designed to serve for the presentation of the drama the same functions as the ordinal served in the daily ceremonial life of the church or chantry. Truncated supplements containing parts or staging directions may have existed,[10] and the term *ordinale* would then distinguish the master copy from such fragments.

In the *Origo Mundi,* when David has been reprimanded by the angel Gabriel for his behavior with Bathsheba and his betrayal of her husband Uriah, a Latin rubric directs, "et tunc sub arbore scā [scientiae] incipit psalterium, scilicet 'Beatus vir' " (And then beneath the tree of knowledge he begins the Psalter; "Blessed is the man") (*OM* 2254).[11] The dramatist handily avails himself of David's penitential attitude to remind his audience that the king was also the psalmist. Yet it may be remarked as well that the systematic rehearsal of the Psalter formed the basis of the canonical hours. Therefore, even though David presents himself dramatically as the composer of the psalms by setting out to say or sing the first verse of the first psalm, his Latin words inevitably recall the clergy assembled in the choir to begin the elaborate program of daily worship that had, chiefly under the influence of the monastic orders, eventually grown up about the Mass.

A more specific echo of the liturgy occurs in the *Resurrexio Domini,* when at the moment of the resurrection the rubric orders, "cantant angeli christus resurgens" (The angels sing *Christus resurgens*) (*RD* 422). *Christus resurgens* was a popular antiphon, "sung in the Salisbury rite when the *Corpus Domini* and the Rood were brought away from the Easter Sepulchre" [12] on Easter Day. The text was used not only in this symbolic and colorful procession before the Mass on Easter, but was also frequently repeated throughout the season from Easter to the ascension, sometimes as a sequence and at least once as the communion (*feria iv post pascha*) and as a processional antiphon: "Christus resurgens ex mortuis iam non moritur mors illi ultra non dominabitur quod enim uiuit uiuit deo alleluia alleluia." (Christ, rising from the dead, dies not and death will have no more dominion over him, for he lives indeed, he lives in God—alleluia, alleluia.) [13]

Specific directions are given for this procession in the ordinal established by Bishop Grandisson in 1337 for use in the cathedral of Exeter and throughout his diocese.[14] Since Cornwall fell within this diocese, and more particularly because of the close ties between the collegiate establishment of Glasney and the cathedral chapter at Exeter, this usage may be presumed shortly to have become general. Because the date corresponds roughly to the earliest suggested date for the *Ordinalia,* one wishes for some firm liturgical evidence in the plays to fix them either before or after Grandisson's effort at ceremonial unification, but what there is seems rather flimsy. The Exeter Ordinal is, in fact, based on the use of Sarum, which is thought to have been the general standard throughout Britain. Information about liturgical customs in Cornwall before Grandisson, however, seems to indicate a considerable degree of local variation.[15]

Immediately after his resurrection Jesus discovers his mother engaged in a tender lament for the slain son whom she presumes dead and for whose restoration she begs. Jesus greets her with the Latin tag, "o salue sancta parens" (*RD* 455). This expression is best known as the opening words of a hymn taken from a poem by the fifth century writer Sedulius which became generally used in the introit for votive Masses of the Blessed Virgin: [16]

> Salve, sancta parens, enixa puerpera regem,
> Qui caelum terramque tenet per saecula, cuius
> Nomen et aeterno complectens omnia gyro.

(Hail, holy mother, who brought forth the king who rules the heavens and the earth forever and whose name embraces all things in their eternal rounds.) [17]

In the *Resurrexio Domini,* at the ascension, after Jesus has properly identified himself to the puzzled angels, one of them proclaims,

ny ny tywyn ow cane
Gloria in excelsis deo.

(Let us not be silent, singing *gloria in excelsis Deo: RD* 2527–
2528.) The rubric immediately following accordingly directs, "tunc
cantant omnes angeli Gloria in excelsis deo." The song that all the
angels sing at this juncture is one of the oldest hymns of the Church,
is imitative of the Psalter, and has for its opening the song the
angels are said to have sung at the nativity (Luke 2:14):

> Gloria in excelsis Deo, et in terra pax hominibus bonae voluntatis.
> Laudamus te. Benedicimus te. Adoramus te. Glorificamus te. Gratias
> agimus tibi, propter magnam gloriam tuam: Domine Deus, Rex
> coelestis, Deus Pater omnipotens. Domine, Fili unigenite, Jesu Christe:
> Domine Deus, Agnus Dei, Filius Patris: Qui tollis peccata mundi,
> miserere nobis. Qui tollis peccata mundi, suscipe deprecationem nos-
> tram. Qui sedes ad dexteram Patris, miserere nobis. Quoniam tu solus
> Sanctus, tu solus Dominus, tu solus altissimus, Jesu Christe: Cum sancto
> Spiritu, in gloria Dei Patris, Amen.

(Glory to God in the highest, and on earth peace to men of good
will. We praise thee, we bless thee, we adore thee, we glorify thee.
We give thee thanks for thy great glory. Lord God, heavenly King,
God the Father almighty. Lord Jesus Christ, the only-begotten Son.
Lord God, Lamb of God, Son of the Father, who takest away the
sins of the world, have mercy upon us. Thou who takest away the
sins of the world, receive our prayer. Thou who sittest at the right
hand of the Father, have mercy upon us. For thou only art holy.
Thou only art Lord. Thou only, O Jesus Christ, with the Holy
Spirit, art most high in the glory of God the Father. Amen.) [18]
    This hymn made its way gradually into the Mass, although
like the *Te Deum* it had always been very popular as a kind of
festival piece. It falls between the *kyrie* and the collect at the opening of Mass, and although it might be associated particularly with
Christmas, it belonged rather more to the festive mood than to any
festive season of the church: its use is discontinued between Septuagesima and Easter. Its appearance at the ascension is therefore
at once liturgically and dramatically effective. The fact that the

hymn is sung by the seven angels recalls the careful ceremonial directions given by Bishop Grandisson of Exeter for its singing at Christmas by seven boys.[19] I should not wish to overemphasize the numerical difference between Sarum and Exeter, but in the Sarum use only five boys represented the angel choir. In the *Ordinalia* the parts of the seven angels at the ascension were very likely taken by the same seven boys who play the *pueri hebreorum* at the beginning of the *Passio Christi.*

This phrase, *pueri hebreorum,* used in the *Passio Christi* to describe the children who welcome Jesus' entry into Jerusalem and his procession to the temple, is taken from one of the antiphons sung when palms are distributed on Palm Sunday.[20] The tag itself is used in the rubric following line 228 and is translated in line 239 as *fleghes ebbrow.* The boys utter a translated version of the last phrase of one antiphon, "Pueri hebreorum uestimenta pros-ternebant in uia et clamabant dicentes osanna filio dauid benedictus qui uenit in nomine domini":

> bynyges yv map a ras
> yn hanow dev devethys.

(Blessed is the son of grace, come in the name of God: *PC* 253–254; cf. 274–276.) The phrase is taken from the Bible (Matthew 21:9, Mark 11:10, John 21:13).

Jenner suggests that the various speeches with which the boys greet Jesus are based on the famous Palm Sunday processional hymn, *Gloria, laus et honor,* by Theodulph, Bishop of Orleans (ca. 750–821).[21] The association is not unlikely, particularly in view of the direction in the Sarum rite that the antiphon is to be sung by seven boys—in this case, the numerical specification appears to be peculiar to Sarum—*in eminenti loco* (in a high place): [22] there are also seven boys specified in the *Ordinalia.* Young, on the other hand, points out the popularity of a medieval custom of "bringing into the church of a figure representing Christ riding on an ass," [23] a ceremonial with which the antiphon *Pueri hebreorum* was also associated.

With regard to these hymnodic examples from the Cornish *Ordinalia,* it is appropriate to remark the observation of one writer that the "antiphonal chanting of a monastic or cathedral choir . . . long continued to serve as a unifying force in the [medieval] plays, integrating the various little scenes by lyrical commentary and filling the pauses in the action with familiar antiphons or hymns related to the liturgy of the occurring feast." [24] On the other hand, not every reminiscence of church music in the *Ordinalia* is so simply pious. In the *Origo Mundi,* as the two devils, Beelzebub and Satan, prepare to carry off Abel to hell, Satan advises his comrade:

> Dun ganso the dre warnot
> th'agan arluth lucifer
> my a gan an conternot
> ha ty dyscant ym-kener.

(Come with him home speedily to our lord Lucifer: I will sing the counter note, and you shall sing discant with me: *OM* 559– 562.)

While the song the devils sing is not given, the indication of an infernal proficiency in the techniques of medieval polyphony is clearly satirical, and may be aimed at an increasing tendency toward elaboration and ornamentation in musical performance within the liturgy. The melodic line is noticeably absent from this assignation of parts, since both the counter note and discant were parts used for harmonic elaboration.[25] A very early instance of two-part music survives in a twelfth century Cornish manuscript (MS. Bodley 572) and is, according to Gustave Reese, "among the earliest practical examples of contrary motion that we have." [26]

The Latin phrases that from time to time punctuate the dialogue of the *Ordinalia* constitute another liturgical echo. Even a biblical quotation in Latin might well recall to the auditor rather the liturgical setting in which he had heard it quoted than the scriptural setting from which it came. Moses' dying utterance, "in manus tuas domine" (*OM* 1898; cf. Luke 23:46), may have just such an effect, although I have discussed it in other terms above (see p. 31). Thus, too, the rubric at the mocking of Jesus, directing the torturer to shout "Aue rex Judeorum" (*PC* 2530; cf. Matthew 27:29, Mark 15:18, John 19:3); the cry "crucifige" (*PC* 2476; cf. Mark 15:13,14, Luke 23:21, John 19:6, 10,15); [27] the rubric "mulier noli me tangere" (*RD* 874; cf. John 20:17); and the phrase used by the pilgrims to Emmaus, "literas nobis in via" (*RD* 1326; cf. Luke 24:32): though all these tags are biblical, all are at the same time mimetic of if not specifically associated with the Latin ritual.

More obviously reminiscent of the divine services, of course, are the phrases that are specifically characteristic of and occur in the liturgy. Just before he begins the Psalter, David utters the ejaculation "Deus mei miserere"—God have mercy on me (*OM* 2252). Again, as he sets out to retrieve the rods of which the wood of the cross will be fashioned, David's macaronic prayer is ritually allusive:

> In nomine dei patris
> a nef mennaf yskynne
> ejus atque spiritus
> re worro wyth am ene.

(*In nomine Dei patris* [in the name of God the father] of heaven, I will mount, *ejus atque spiritus* [and may his spirit] set a guard over my soul: *OM* 1975–1978.) Adam uses part of the phrase (*OM* 666), and later David uses what is basically the same formulaic tag to heal three unfortunates with the miraculous rods:

> In nomine dei patris et filii
> atque spiritus sancti
> salui modo eritis.

(In the name of God the father and the son and the Holy Spirit, you will now be healed: *OM* 2020–2022.)

Now that he has found the emblematically trinitarian rods, David is apparently able to use the full trinitarian formula itself. The phrase is taken from Jesus' parting words to his disciples (Matthew 28:19), and had become the fundamental text invoking

blessing throughout the ceremonies of the church. The variation in
the *Ordinalia* from the usual form, "in nomine patris," is slight,
but it was used, for example, in exorcisms, and can at any rate be
explained simply on rhythmic grounds. Jesus himself uses the
phrase on a similar occasion:

> In nomine patris et filii
> et spiritus sancti amen.
> Transite a me sani.

(In the name of the father and the son and the Holy Spirit, amen.
Go forth from me healed: *PC* 405–407.)

David's fondness for these liturgical Latin ejaculations can be
accounted for, as I have indicated with his chanting of the Psalter,
as efforts to associate him with the ritual of which his psaltery
formed so important and striking a part. The phrase "bene dicite
dominus," ascribed to David upon his awakening from the dream in
which the angel Gabriel had instructed him to seek for the three
rods (*OM* 1953), is probably misinterpreted by Norris: it very
likely represents an interjection based on the traditional formula for
beseeching a blessing, "benedicite." As he blurts out these words,
David is no doubt protecting himself from any conceivable demonic
influence on his dream-troubled sleep.

Another catchword from the liturgy occurs when Pilate discovers the disappearance of Joseph and Nicodemus from prison,
and threatens the jailers rather elliptically:

> mar ny's cafaf scon thu'm dues
> ty a fyth drok oremus.

(If I do not find them soon come to me, you shall have an evil
oremus: RD 648.) The word "oremus" is simply a summons to
prayer, and naturally occurs frequently in the liturgy. It became
associated with the prayers that it introduced, and was used to
denote such prayers. Pilate is therefore simply invoking the prospect
of a "bad prayer" on his underlings, and his imprecation is only
very faintly, if at all, redolent of the ritual.

The material thus far treated comprises the overt reminiscence

of the liturgy in the *Ordinalia.* In sum, it is curiously uninstructive
and unproductive. The auditor would have been reminded occasionally by scraps out of the rites to which he was more or less
accustomed that the church with its ceremony was involved in what
he saw, but those few hints are hardly sufficient to have led him
to an appreciably deepened affinity for or knowledge of the relationship between the biblical and the eucharistic drama. Even the few
hints provided are not systematically introduced nor are they always—with the remarkable exception of the processional antiphons
—symbolically clear.

If, on the other hand, the liturgical intention of a pedagogic
dramatist was to instruct his audience in the nature and manner of
worship, the *Ordinalia* provides rather more puzzlement than eluci-
dation in its treatment of ceremonial worship within the plays. The
sacrifice of Cain and Abel or of Noah and his family or even of
Abraham are essentially acts of public worship, like the services of
the church, but they are not even remotely liturgical and are only
very simply ceremonial as set down in the *Ordinalia.* Likewise the
mockery of Christ is a kind of travesty of worship, but it cannot
accurately be called either instructive or satirical, whether by intent
or in effect.

Nonetheless, if the various echoes of the liturgy in the *Ordinalia* do not individually or cumulatively point to a general concept
involved in the daily services of the church, they do reinforce a
much larger liturgical scheme to be seen within the drama as a
whole. Hardin Craig insists that the religious drama of the Middle
Ages "was closely bound from beginning to end by the doctrines
of the church particularly as embodied in the cursus of the liturgical
year in the form of lections or pericopes," [28] and the shape of the
liturgical year is clearly discernible in the *Ordinalia.*

Although the Mass and other offices of the church do not
undergo any essential alterations in form or function from day to
day or from season to season, several variable characteristics are
introduced both into the Mass and into the calendar of feasts and

services as the year passes, in order to emphasize or to celebrate certain events within the experience of the church. Every Mass, therefore, is fundamentally an unvarying repetition of the eucharistic sacrifice. But certain prayers, hymns, lessons, and responses do change from day to day as the church observes particular times and seasons. Within the cycle of seasonal emphases running from Advent to Advent, the period that is most significant for the medieval drama in general and for the *Ordinalia* in particular begins with Septuagesima and ends with Pentecost. Commemoratively, "the object of this period is the whole of sacred history, the whole mystery of Christ and of the Church, under the aspect of Redemption." [29] The emphasis within Septuagesima falls on the Old Testament preparation for and prefiguration of Christ; the season of Lent recalls his ministry, and Holy Week, his passion; Easter celebrates his resurrection; the ascension affirms that the work of redemption is successfully accomplished; and Pentecost remembers the institution and perpetuation of the redemptive activity among men and within the church.

The *Ordinalia* is modeled on this same commemorative scheme. Beginning with the creation and proceeding to the ascension, it deals serially with the liturgical events of the developing seasons, saving notably the interpolated material from the legend of the cross and the death of Pilate. Indeed, fidelity to this liturgical plan no doubt further helps to explain the omission from the *Ordinalia* of those scenes from the nativity that were so popular elsewhere: they belong to a liturgical season, Advent, that does not fit into the episodic sequence of the plays. Thus, historically appropriate though they would have been in a strictly biblical sequence, their liturgical displacement justifies their absence. In their stead, the temptation of Christ is used, as it is used liturgically in the beginning of Lent, to deal with the transition from the prefiguration to the reality of incarnation.

The connection between the Old Testament plays and the season beginning at Septuagesima has been established and discussed elsewhere.[30] Septuagesima includes the three Sundays that immediately precede Ash Wednesday and the beginning of Lent, and are usually decimally distinguished in the calendar as Septuagesima, Sexagesima, and Quinquagesima. The Sundays in this season give particular attention, successively, to the stories in Genesis of the creation and fall, Noah and the ark, and the sacrifice of Abraham.[31] The same stories constitute the opening episodes of *Origo Mundi* in the Cornish plays. Although, as the names of the three Sundays would suggest, this pre-Lenten season was a relatively late development in the seasonal cycle of church usage,[32] it was firmly established in the calendar well before the earliest surviving evidences of liturgical drama appeared.

If we may ignore, for the moment, the problem of the intervening period, the next subject treated in the *Ordinalia* is the history of Moses. The material thus dealt with appears in various readings on "Laetare" Sunday, the fourth in Lent, and during the following week. What remains of the Old Testament matter in the *Ordinalia* deals with David and Solomon, and therefore has nothing to do with the scriptural readings proper to the season.[33] On the other hand, both kings figure prominently in the legend of the cross, which helps to justify their presence in the drama.

Nearly all the events dealt with in the *Passio Christi* have their place in the ceremonies of Holy Week itself. The story of the Passion, which constitutes the events beginning with the arrest and leading to the death of Jesus, is read as the gospel four times during the week, once from each of the evangelical books. The same story is the basis of this second day's play in the *Ordinalia*. Even the preparatory material, however, has its place in the various ritual activities of this most important week in the church's liturgical year.

The *Passio Christi* begins with the temptation of Jesus by the devil. This scene serves, as I have suggested, both to establish the theme of the incarnation—since it constitutes an effort on the devil's part to try whether Jesus be god or man—and to recapitulate the penitential emphasis of the Quadragesimal season of which Holy Week is the climax. The story itself is read during the lessons of the first Sunday in Lent.

The relationship of the subsequent episode—the entry of Jesus into Jerusalem and his procession to the temple—to Palm Sunday with its own festive procession is sufficiently obvious to require no elaboration. The following episodes recall the ceremonies of Maundy Thursday. Mary Magdalene anoints Jesus' feet with oil and receives Jesus' blessing when Judas rebukes her for extravagance. This interlude is strongly reminiscent of the ceremonial blessing of the holy oils and chrism during the Mass of Maundy Thursday. In this rite the oils that will be used in baptism and other anointings are consecrated by the bishop.

The Last Supper, prototype of the eucharistic celebration on this day as on every other—save Good Friday, when alone it is not celebrated—follows, and is followed by Jesus' washing the feet of his disciples. This ceremonial foot-washing is regarded as the institution of the *mandatum,* a liturgical re-enactment and perpetuation of Jesus' self-abasement from which the English term for the day, "maundy," derives.[34]

The subsequent events belong to the Passion proper and can be found in the various gospels. The resurrection is, of course, celebrated on Easter Sunday, and the several subsequent episodes are all commemorated in the lessons and chants during the week following Easter—Jesus' appearance to Mary Magdalene, to the apostles, to two disciples (*peregrinatio*) on the road to Emmaus, and lastly to the doubting Thomas. Again, the *Mors Pilati* is a disruptive interpolation in the *Ordinalia,* for the legend does not belong to the liturgy of the season. The plays end with the ascension, an event liturgically commemorated in a great church festival on the fortieth day after Easter.

Fundamentally, then, the drama shapes itself with astonishing correspondence to the seasonal procession of the liturgy. While, to be sure, the church year observes a commemoratively historical pattern itself throughout this period, the most striking correspondence between liturgy and drama can be discerned in their respective emphases. Both the drama and the liturgy are more or less faithful to scriptural chronology, yet the two share more characteristic emphases in choosing from this material than sheer coincidence would permit. Because of this affinity, and in light of the studies by Young, Craig, Kretzmann, and others that deal with the various liturgical origins of the drama, a principal question remains to be treated. The liturgy of Holy Week produced the seminal drama from which the vernacular cycles developed, and the Old Testament plays can be seen reflected in the *responsoria* of Septuagesima. To what extent, therefore, is the vernacular drama a simple product of its liturgical origins and to what extent does it seek self-consciously to be liturgically instructive? The question is, of course, unduly speculative and, to some degree, establishes an artificial distinction. Nonetheless, such an inquiry may within limits be profitable.

One of the most understandably popular episodes in the dramatic cycles was the Harrowing of Hell play. Kretzmann associated this recapitulation of Christ's triumphant liberation of the patriarchs from infernal bondage during the time between his death and resurrection with the liturgical emphases of the "Great Sabbath," or the day before Easter. He concluded that "there is something in all vernacular plays, except the Cornish, that points to liturgical source or influence" [35] on this particular episode. He need not, in fact, have excepted the *Ordinalia:* although the injunction to "open the gates" retains none of the usual Latin tags (based on Psalms 24), the powerful and memorable dialogue is translated and given without much elaboration in Cornish.[36]

The attention given the Harrowing of Hell on the day before Easter was no mere accident, nor was it an episode designed simply to fill a lacuna between the crucifixion and the resurrection. Its historic associations are rather with the liturgical event that is marked on Holy Saturday. The Vigil of the Resurrection is, in fact, the most solemn and climactic of all the services in the church,[37] for the focus of this liturgical observance is historically the rite of Christian baptism. During the several centuries before the church began generally to practice infant baptism, the Vigil of Easter was the yearly occasion for the solemn initiation of catechumens into the mysteries and ceremonies of the faith. The Harrowing of Hell was the supremely dramatic type of the liberation effected by such baptism.

In time, the centrality of this baptismal occasion in the liturgical activities of the church was eroded by the growing practice of infant baptism: when membership in the community of faith became, in effect, a birthright, it was but natural that it should be conferred at birth. Baptism, then, could be administered throughout the year, and its association with the single occasion on the eve of Easter was diminished. The office, however, did not disappear from the liturgy, and the church asked finally that any babies born within eight days of Holy Saturday be denied baptism until the traditional rites could be employed during the Vigil.[38]

The association between this baptismal event and the Harrowing of Hell recalls that the liturgical framework for the entire season of preparation was laid while baptism, and its conferral upon the catechumens who had received prior instruction in the meaning and mysteries of faith, were culminating events in the worship of the church. Indeed, Quadragesima apparently began as a season of instructional and spiritual preparation for aspiring communicants, and only became essentially penitential when this habit of induction was, in the main, lost. Nonetheless, the fundamental instructional pattern was not abandoned. If the period beginning with Septuagesima in the church's calendar sought to recapitulate the history of the redemption, it did so at least ultimately with the intention of guiding the real or hypothetical neophyte through the ground plan of his faith.

A recognition that this liturgical season was originally intended to prepare catechumens for receiving the sacrament of baptism can be seen, for example, in Hugh of St. Victor who, about 1134, could write of "those lately converted to the faith" that they

are to be instructed in the visible sacraments . . . [They] should be advised to consider that the faith is not new in which they themselves are new, since, just as from the beginning of the world at no time were the faithful and the just lacking as members of Christ, so from the beginning never have the sacraments of salvation which preceded for the preparation and for the sign of the redemption which was completed in the death of Christ been lacking. [For in the first age Abel offered a lamb for a sacrifice, a figure of the death of Christ.] In the second age Noah guided the ark in the flood, just as Christ guiding the Church midst the floods of temptations did not permit it to be submerged. In the third age Abraham slaughtered a ram for his son who had been offered, just as God the Father offered His Word for the salvation of the world . . . Afterwards the people of Israel were led out of Egypt through the Red Sea in a column of fire and cloud, just as the faithful of God are freed from the shades of sin, renewed through the sacrament of baptism, consecrated by the blood of Christ, following with faith Him himself in whom is both the cloud of humanity and the fire of divinity. In the fourth age in Jerusalem the temporal kingdom of the people of God is raised, prefiguring the eternal in which the Prince of Peace, the Father of the world to come, will introduce His faithful to the vision of eternal peace. Now David established the beginning of this kingdom, who tried and glorified through many tribulations left the Son as the successor of peace to show that they cannot come to the quiet of future peace who in the present life have not been strong against the trials and tribulations which must be overpowered. On this account, those who are to be baptized on the Holy Sabbath of the paschal solemnity, are brought to the church on the fourth hebdomada of the quadragesimal observance which furnishes us the arms of continence and on the fourth festival of the same hebdomada to be catechized and exorcised, there to hear and to be instructed as to how they are to fight against spiritual wickedness. But their baptism is postponed, even until the Sabbath of the paschal festival, while the Church considers that, in whatever respect they are called to combat in the present life, they are baptized in the hope of future rest.[39]

The historically allusive scheme to which Hugh would direct the neophyte's attention is, of course, embodied in the lectional frame of the pre-Easter season and, even more strikingly, accurately describes the episodic development of the *Ordinalia*. Indeed, whether self-consciously or not, the drama has exploited for its own instructional purposes a scheme ready at hand in the liturgical structure of the church, a scheme that, as Hugh of St. Victor's self-conscious explication makes clear, was intended for other but similar instructional purposes. The *Ordinalia* is, in effect, addressed to an audience of catechumens. The drama does not, to be sure, make this claim for its spectators, since after all the members of the audience would have been properly baptized at birth; yet it was intended to serve an instructional purpose, and what it could best teach about the liturgy, the Lenten liturgy had been designed to teach. The dramatist, therefore, understandably availed himself of the convenient scheme that had been established for just that purpose. One might have expected to find in the plays some demonstrable effort at explaining the often obscurely symbolic activities of the Mass. Instead, they have another sacramental function altogether.

Baptism, of course, is not repeatable in the life of any Christian, and it has always been the symbol *par excellence* of spiritual regeneration in the church. Hugh of St. Victor chooses his baptismal types in order to point out a historically connected prechristian series of sacramental and spiritual renewals directed by God. The *Ordinalia* uses the same events at least partly for the same reasons. The theme of regeneration, after all, is the focal point of the entire drama. Its primacy is evident not only in the Passion and the resurrection, but also in the primarily typological events of the Old Testament. Moreover, the legend of the cross, Thomas' lengthy ordeal of disbelief, and nearly every other episode in the drama, with the outstanding exception of the *Mors Pilati,* shares this same emphasis. That it should be so is not surprising: as Lundberg observes, "What is accomplished in baptism, then, is not a magical transformation of man; rather, it is the application of the redemptive work of Jesus to the person baptized by the establishment of a personal communion between Christ and man." [40]

To trace this theme of renewal through the *Ordinalia* would be merely to reiterate my discussion of the relationship of the Bible to the *Ordinalia,* for both the exegetical scheme and the liturgical emphasis center in the redemption, indeed both treat history and worship from the central affirmation of a redemptive plan culminating in the work of Jesus. The birth of Seth, to take but one example, prefigures Christ; it is also an episode along the way of what Hugh of St. Victor calls the "sacraments of salvation." Several of the biblical and dramatic episodes are traditional types of baptism itself: the flood, for instance, and the crossing of the Red Sea and the Descent into Hell. Yet such sacramental types are but part of the whole scheme of spiritual renewal. The quest of Seth for the oil of mercy is an example of the eschatological or paradisiac manifestation of this plan; Maximilla's martyrdom is prophetic; Longinus' restored sight is eucharistic. Throughout, in one way or another, the drama builds on and intensifies an anticipation of regeneration, the fulfillment of which is Jesus' act of redemption.

The drama therefore constitutes a visual enactment of the devil's struggle for man's soul. If, as I have suggested, the dramatist is not certain precisely how the battle is won, he nevertheless regards victory as its aim, and that victory is redemption. The liturgy is not in the forefront of this battle, but it describes, as it were, the battle plan, and the drama exploits that plan. The biblical cycles are based on the liturgical scheme of the church year as it develops from Septuagesima on; but I suspect that the *Ordinalia,* at any rate, is less the product of a haphazard collation of biblical-liturgical plays than a dramatic achievement that draws on a liturgical program for reasons of its own. The *Ordinalia* is as coherent as the liturgy of this season in the church year because both share a desire for teaching aspirants—the one catechumens, and the other unknowledgeable laymen—to become spiritually knowledgeable participants in the community of faith.

Epilogue

OF ALL THE temptations that beset the critic of medieval drama, none is more persistent and none more treacherous than the urge to make some firm assessment of the drama's artistic merit. For one thing, such an evaluation, if it is to be at all intelligent, requires an understanding of the intentions and artistic assumptions that lie behind the works themselves. Unhappily, however, the Middle Ages produced no Aristotle to act as interpreter or as guide to the perplexed. Therefore, the critic is left hazardously to chart his own way through an alien literary landscape. The fear of going astray or wandering forever in a dark wood has, nonetheless, rarely deterred any critic, and the urge to resolve this particular perplexity is, if anything, probably stronger today than ever before.

Not many students of the drama would any longer be content with the amiable superciliousness that allowed one expansive lecturer to remark apropos of the *Ordinalia* that "our ancestors were in that happy stage in which are still many of our less 'cultured' brothers, and could enjoy and learn lessons from the thing signified, no matter how grotesquely it might be presented." [1] Yet any informed attempt to measure the intrinsic dramatic qualities of the medieval plays must reckon with the apparent clumsiness of their dramatizations. Consequently, in the past critics have inclined either to dismiss the possibility of artistic merit by calling attention to the simply religious character of the drama or to claim that merit on the basis of some real and some imagined virtues that can be emphasized only by ignoring what is clumsy, trite, or even foolish. Neither approach has been entirely convincing, for each fails in the end adequately to explain what the drama intended to be, and therefore fails to explain what it became. The effort to understand precisely what the early dramatists were trying to do is still of crucial importance, and is still receiving considerable attention.[2]

To get at this problem, a study of what the drama sought to teach may be particularly fruitful. After all, however simple piety and artistic yearning may have struggled against one another for dominion in the plays, the capacity to instruct was in the drama from the beginning, and has been generally recognized. The Cornish *Ordinalia* serves to indicate how well, how thoroughly, and within what limitations the drama undertook instruction. This study has attempted, in fact, to suggest that the *Ordinalia* was quite persistently and very capably didactic. The claims both of piety and of artistry can better be illuminated by recognizing the magnitude of that didactic achievement.

Mâle's remark that the medieval cathedral deserves to be thought of as the "Bible of the poor" applies equally well to the drama.[3] Fundamentally, what the medieval spectator saw and heard during the performance of a biblical dramatic cycle was a kind of catechetical explanation of his faith. One enthusiastic cleric proclaims that "what the ancient Attic drama was to the Athenian workman the old Cornish religious drama was to the mediaeval Cornish tinner—a mighty teacher." [4]

William Durandus made a similar point about ecclesiastical ornamentation when he observed that "pictures and ornaments in churches are the lessons and scriptures of the laity." [5] Surely the comparison need not be labored. To succeed as instruction, the plays had to be dramatically effective; but to succeed dramatically, the dramatist had to be sure of what he wished to teach. If the Cornish tinner were to learn about the redemption, the *Ordinalia* would have to be careful how it taught him.

The redemption was, to be sure, the central affirmation of

the spectator's faith. The *Ordinalia* likewise holds that affirmation central and, in its treatment of biblical events, attempts to provide a rudely typological exegesis to support it; the affirmation remains despite the wavering doctrinal uncertainty consequent on the theological currents that swept about it; finally, the drama undertakes the inculcation of spiritual truths based on the redemption in the same fashion that the liturgical patterns once established had prepared for initiation converts to the same sacramental attitude.

David Rogers recalled in about 1609 that the mystery plays had last been performed in Chester in 1574: "And wee have all cause to power out our prayeres before God, that neither wee nor oure posterities after us, maye never see ye like abomination of desolation, with suche a Clowde of Ignorance to defile with so highe a hand ye sacred scriptures of God." [6] Rogers would probably not have appreciated the irony of his remark even had he understood that the plays he condemned had had their roots in a piety as earnest as his own. Howsoever offensive the medieval drama may have been to this child of the Reformation, it was intended not to defile but to reveal those precious mysteries. The Cornish *Ordinalia* is, in fact, a splendid memorial to the pedagogical genius and integrity of the vernacular biblical dramatist who shaped it.

Bibliography

Notes

Index

Bibliography

Anderson, M. D. *Drama and Imagery in English Medieval Churches.* Cambridge, Eng., 1963.

Anselm. *Cur Deus Homo* [tr. James Gardiner Vose], ed. Sidney Norton Deane. La Salle, Illinois, 1951.

Aquinas, St. Thomas. *Summa Theologica,* tr. Fathers of the English Dominican Province. 3 vols. New York, 1947–1948.

Ashton, John, ed. *The Legendary History of the Cross: A Series of Sixty-four Woodcuts from a Dutch Book Published by Veldener, A.D. 1483.* London, 1887.

Auerbach, Erich. "Figura," *Archivum Romanicum,* 22 (1938): 436–489. Reprinted in *Neue Dantestudien* (Istanbul, 1944), pp. 11–71.

———— *Mimesis: The Representation of Reality in Western Literature,* tr. Willard R. Trask. Princeton, 1953.

———— "Typologische Motive in der mittelalterlichen Literatur," *Schriften und Vorträge des Petrarca-Instituts Köln,* vol. II. Krefeld, Germ., 1953.

Augustine. *The City of God,* tr. Marcus Dods. New York, 1950.

Aulén, Gustav. *Christus Victor: An Historical Study of the Three Main Types of the Idea of Atonement,* tr. A. G. Hebert. New York, 1951.

Bainton, Roland H. *Early and Medieval Christianity.* Boston, 1962.

Bede, The Venerable. *Vita sanctorum abbatum monasterii in Uyrmutha et Gyruum,* in J. E. King., ed., *Baedae Opera Historica* (Cambridge, Mass., and London: Loeb Classical Library, 1954), II, 392–445.

Berger, Samuel. *Histoire de la Vulgate pendant les premiers siècles du moyen âge.* Paris, 1893.

Berjeau, J. Ph., ed. *Geschiedenis van het heylighe Cruys; or, History of the Holy Cross: Reproduced in Facsimile from the Original Edition Printed by J. Veldener in 1483.* London, 1863.

Bernard, J. H. *Studia Sacra.* London, 1917.

Bloomfield, Morton W. "Symbolism in Medieval Literature," *Modern Philology,* 56 (1958): 73–81.

Boehner, Philotheus, ed. "The *Centiloquium* Attributed to Ockham," *Franciscan Studies,* vols. XXII–XXIII (1941–42), in six parts, pp. 58–72 *et passim.*

Bonaventure. *Collationes in Hexaemeron,* ed. Ferdinandus Delorme. Florence, 1934.

Borde, Andrew. *The Fyrst Boke of the Introduction of Knowledge,* ed. F. J. Furnivall. London: EETS, 1870.

Borlase, William. *Antiquities, Historical and Monumental, of the County of Cornwall.* 2nd ed. London, 1769.

——— *The Natural History of Cornwall.* Oxford, 1758.

Bouyer, Louis. *The Paschal Mystery,* tr. Sr. Mary Benoit. London, 1951.

Brooks, Neil C. *The Sepulchre of Christ in Art and Liturgy.* Urbana, Illinois: University of Illinois Studies in Language and Literature (VII), 1921.

Brown, Raymond Edward. *The 'Sensus Plenior' of Sacred Scripture.* Baltimore, 1955.

Brugger, E. *The Illuminated Tree in Two Arthurian Romances.* New York: Institute of French Studies, 1929.

Burkhard, Arthur. "The Isenheim Altar," *Speculum,* 9 (1934): 56–69.

Callewaert, C. "L'Oeuvre liturgique de S. Grégoire: la septuagésime et l'alleluia," *Revue d'histoire ecclésiastique,* 33 (1937): 306–326.

Campanile, Enrico. "Un Frammento scenico medio-cornico," *Studi e saggi linguistici* (Supplement to *L'Italia Dialettale,* vol. 26), 3 (1963): 60–80.

Caplan, Harry. "The Four Senses of Scriptural Interpretation and the Mediaeval Theory of Preaching," *Speculum,* 4 (1929): 282–290.

Carew, Richard (of Antony). *The Survey of Cornwall,* ed. F. E. Halliday. London, 1953.

Cargill, Oscar. *Drama and Liturgy.* New York, 1930.

Carter, Henry Holland. *A Dictionary of Middle English Musical Terms.* Bloomington, Ind., 1961.

Cawley, A. C., ed. *The Wakefield Pageants in the Towneley Cycle.* Manchester, 1958.

Chambers, E. K. *The Mediaeval Stage.* 2 vols. Oxford, 1903.

Chenu, M.-D. "Théologie symbolique et exégèse scolastique aux XIIe–XIIIe siècles," *Mélanges Joseph de Ghellinck, S.J.* (Gembloux, Belg., 1951), II, 509–526.

Chevalier, Ulysse. *Repertorium Hymnologicum.* 6 vols. Louvain, 1897–1912; Brussels, 1920–21.

Clerck, D. E. de. "Droits du démon et nécessité de la rédemption: les écoles d' Abélard et de Pierre Lombard," *Recherches de Théologie ancienne et médiévale,* 14 (1947): 32–64.

Cohen, Gustave. *Etudes d'histoire du théâtre en France au moyen-age et à la Renaissance.* Paris, 1956.

Corpus Scriptorum Ecclesiasticorum Latinorum. Vienna, 1866 et seq.

Craig, Hardin. *English Religious Drama of the Middle Ages.* Oxford, 1955.

—— "The Origin of the Old Testament Plays," *Modern Philology,* 10 (1912–13): 473–487.

—— review of Arnold Williams, *The Drama of Mediaeval England* (q.v.), *Speculum,* 36 (1961): 695–698.

Cross, F. L., ed. *The Oxford Dictionary of the Christian Church.* London, 1957.

Cullman, Oscar. *Christ and Time: The Primitive Christian Conception of Time and History,* tr. Floyd V. Filson. 3rd ed. London, 1962.

Dalton, J. N., ed. *Ordinale Exon.* 4 vols. London: Henry Bradshaw Society, 1909–1940.

Daniel, Hermann Adalbert. *Thesaurus Hymnologicus.* 5 vols. Leipzig, 1855–1856.

Daniélou, Jean. *From Shadows to Reality: Studies in the Biblical Typology of the Fathers,* tr. Wulstan Hibberd. Westminster, Md., 1960.

Dawson, Christopher. *Medieval Essays.* London and New York, 1953.

Deimling, Hermann, and [?] Matthews, edd. *The Chester Plays.* 2 vols. London: EETS, 1893–1916.

Delporte, Lucien. "Les Principes de la typologie biblique et les éléments figuratifs du Sacrifice de l'Expiation," *Ephemerides Theologicae Lovanienses,* 3 (1926): 307–327.

Dibdin, Thomas Frognall. *Bibliotheca Spenceriana.* 4 vols. London, 1814–1815.

Dickinson, Francis Henry, ed. *Missale ad Usum Insignis et Praeclarae Ecclesiae Sarum.* Oxford and London, 1861–1883.

Dictionnaire d'archéologie chrétienne et de liturgie, ed. Fernand Cabrol. 15 vols. Paris, 1903–1953.

Dictionnaire de théologie catholique, ed. A. Vacant, E. Mangenot, and E. Amann. 15 vols. Paris, 1923–1950.

Didron, Alphonse Napoléon. *Christian Iconography; or, The History of Christian Art in the Middle Ages,* tr. E. J. Millington. 2 vols. London, 1851–1886.

Dionysius the Areopagite. *The Works of Dionysius the Areopagite,* tr. John Parker. 2 vols. London and Oxford, 1899.

Donne, John. *Devotions upon Emergent Occasions,* ed. John Sparrow. Cambridge, Eng., 1923.

Dreves, Guido Maria, ed. *Analecta hymnica Medii Aevi.* 55 vols. Leipzig, 1886–1922.

Du Cange, Charles Du Fresne. *Glossarium mediae et infimae latinitatis.* New ed. 10 vols. Paris, 1937–1938.

Duchesne, L. *Christian Worship: Its Origin and Evolution,* tr. M. L. McClure. 4th ed. London, 1912.

Dunn, E. Catherine. "The Medieval 'Cycle' as History Play: an Approach to the Wakefield Plays," *Studies in the Renaissance,* 7 (1960): 76–89.

——— "Lyrical Form and the Prophetic Principle in the Towneley Plays," *Mediaeval Studies,* 23 (1961): 80–90.

Durandus, William. *Rationale divinorum officiorum,* ed. V. d'Avino. Naples, 1859.

Edwards, Kathleen. *The English Secular Cathedrals in the Middle Ages.* Manchester, 1949.

Ehrensperger, Harold. *Religious Drama: Ends and Means.* New York and Nashville, Tenn., 1962.

Elliott-Binns, L. E. *Medieval Cornwall.* London, 1955.

Erbe, Theodor, ed. *Mirk's Festial: A Collection of Homilies, by Johannes Mirkus.* London: EETS, 1905.

Feasey, Henry John. *Ancient English Holy Week Ceremonial.* London, 1897.

Fisher, J. D. C. *Christian Initiation: Baptism in the Medieval West.* London, 1965.

Fitch, Robert, ed. *Norwich Pageants: The Grocers' Play.* Norwich, 1856.

Fortescue, Adrian. *The Ceremonies of the Roman Rite Described.* 7th ed., rev. J. O'Connell. London, 1943.

Foster, Frances A., ed. *The Northern Passion.* 2 vols. London: EETS, 1913–1916.

——— ed. *A Stanzaic Life of Christ Compiled from Higden's Polychronicon and the Legenda Aurea.* London: EETS, 1926.

Foster, Joseph, ed. *Alumni Oxonienses: The Members of the University of Oxford, 1500–1714.* 4 vols. London, 1891–1892.

Fowler, David C. *Piers the Plowman: Literary Relations of the A and B Texts.* Seattle, Washington, 1961.

——— "The Date of the Cornish *Ordinalia,*" *Mediaeval Studies,* 23 (1961): 91–125.

Frank, Grace. *The Medieval French Drama.* Oxford and New York, 1954.

——— "Vernacular Sources and an Old French Passion Play," *Modern Language Notes,* 35 (1920): 257–269.

Frank, Robert Worth, Jr. *Piers Plowman and the Scheme of Salvation: An Interpretation of 'Dowel, Dobet, and Dobest'.* New Haven, 1957.

Franks, Robert S. *The Atonement.* London, 1934.

—————— *A History of the Doctrine of the Work of Christ in Its Ecclesiastical Development.* 2nd ed. Edinburgh, 1962.

Frere, Walter Howard. *A Collection of His Papers on Liturgical and Historical Subjects.* London: Alcuin Club Collections, 1940.

—————— ed. *The Use of Sarum.* 2 vols. Cambridge, Eng., 1898–1901.

Frolow, A. *La Relique de la vraie croix.* Paris, 1961.

Fry, Timothy. "The Unity of the *Ludus Coventriae*," *Studies in Philology,* 48 (1951): 527–570.

Füglister, Robert Louis. *Das Lebende Kreuz: ikonographisch-ikonologische Untersuchung der Herkunft und Entwicklung einer spät-mittelalterlichen Bildidee und ihrer Verwurzelung im Wort.* Einsiedeln, 1964.

Furnivall, F. J., ed. *The Digby Plays.* London: EETS, 1896.

Gaffney, Wilbur. "The Allegory of the Christ-Knight in *Piers Plowman*," *PMLA,* 46 (1931): 155–168.

Gaster, Moses. *Ilchester Lectures on Greeko-Slavonic Literature.* London, 1887.

Gayley, Charles Mills. *Plays of our Forefathers.* New York, 1907.

Geiriadur Prifysgol Cymru: A Dictionary of the Welsh Language, ed. R. J. Thomas. Cardiff, 1950 *et seq.*

Gilbert, Davies, ed. *The Creation of the World, with Noah's Flood; Written in Cornish in the Year 1611, by William Jordan,* tr. John Keigwin. London, 1827.

—————— *The Parochial History of Cornwall, Founded on the Manuscript Histories of Mr. Hals and Mr. Tonkin.* 4 vols. London, 1838.

Gilson, Etienne. *The Mystical Theology of Saint Bernard,* tr. A. H. C. Downes. London, 1940.

—————— *The Philosophy of St. Bonaventure,* tr. Illtyd Trethowan and F. J. Sheed. New York, 1938.

Glunz, H. H. *History of the Vulgate in England from Alcuin to Roger Bacon.* Cambridge, Eng., 1933.

Goodman, Hadassah Posey. *Original Elements in the French and German Passion Plays: A Study of the Passion Scenes.* Bryn Mawr, Penn., 1944.

Goppelt, Leonhard. *Typos. Die typologische Deutung des Alten Testaments im Neuen.* Gütersloh: *Beiträge zur Förderung Christlicher Theologie,* ed. Adolf Schlatter and Paul Althaus, II (43), 1939.

Graduale Sarisburiense, ed. W. H. Frere. London: Plain Song and Mediaeval Music Society, 1894.

Grant, Robert M. *The Letter and the Spirit.* London, 1957.

—————— *A Short History of the Interpretation of the Bible,* rev. ed. New York, 1963.

Graves, Eugene Van Tassel. "The Old Cornish Vocabulary." Doctoral dissertation, Columbia University, 1962.

Grensted, L. W. *A Short History of the Doctrine of the Atonement.* Manchester, 1920.

Guéranger, Prosper. *L'Année liturgique.* 16 vols. Paris and elsewhere, 1868 *et seq.*

Gwreans an Bys. See Davies Gilbert; Whitley Stokes.

Gwryans an Bys, ed. R. Morton Nance and A. S. D. Smith. Federation of Old Cornwall Societies, n.d.: mimeograph.

Halliday, F. E., ed. and tr. *The Legend of the Rood.* London, 1955.

Harbage, Alfred. *Annals of English Drama, 975–1700,* rev. S. Schoenbaum. London and Philadelphia, 1964.

Hardison, O. B., Jr. *Christian Rite and Christian Drama in the Middle Ages: Essays in the Origin and Early History of Modern Drama.* Baltimore, 1965.

Hardy, Edward Rochie, ed. *Christology of the Later Fathers.* Philadelphia: The Library of Christian Classics, 1954.

Harris, Phyllis Pier, ed. and tr. *"Origo Mundi,* First Play of the Cornish Mystery Cycle, the *Ordinalia:* A New Edition." Doctoral dissertation, University of Washington, 1964.

Hastings, James, ed. *A Dictionary of the Bible.* 5 vols. New York, 1898–1904.

Hedgeland, J. P. *A Description, Accompanied by Sixteen Coloured Plates, of the Splendid Decorations Recently Made to the Church of St. Neot in Cornwall.* London, 1830.

Henderson, Charles. *The Ecclesiastical History of Western Cornwall.* 2 vols. Truro, Eng., 1962.

Henderson, W. G., ed. *Processionale ad usum insignis ac praeclarae ecclesiae Sarum.* Leeds, 1882.

Herr, Jeanne Lucien. "La Reine de Saba et le bois de la croix," *Revue archéologique,* 4th series, 23 (1914): 1–31.

Heuser, Wilhelm, and Frances A. Foster, edd. *The Northern Passion (Supplement).* London: EETS, 1930.

Higden, Ranulph. *Polychronicon Ranulphi Higden Monachi Cestrensis; together with the English Translations of John Trevisa and of an Unknown Writer of the Fifteenth Century,* ed. Churchill Babington and Joseph Rawson Lumby. 9 vols. London: Rolls Series 41, 1865–1886.

Hill, Betty. "The Fifteenth-Century Prose *Legend of the Cross before Christ,*" *Medium Aevum,* 34 (1965): 203–222.

Hilton, H. H., Jr., ed. *"Seth,* an Anglo-Norman Poem," *Studies in the Romance Lauguages and Literatures,* 2 (1941): 41–61.

Holmstedt, Gustaf, ed. *Speculum Christiani: A Middle English Religious Treatise of the 14th Century.* London: EETS, 1933.

Hope, W. H. St. John, ed. *English Altars from Illuminated Manu-scripts*. London: Alcuin Club Collections, 1899.

Horstmann, Carl. *The Early South-English Legendary or Lives of Saints*. London: EETS, 1887.

—— "Nachträge zu den Legenden," *Archiv für das Studium der neueren Sprachen und Litteraturen*, 79 (1887): 411–470.

—— *Sammlung altenglischer Legenden*. Heilbronn, Germ., 1878.

Hort, Greta. *Piers Plowman and Contemporary Religious Thought*. London, n.d.

Hugh of St. Victor. *The Didascalion*, ed. and tr. Jerome Taylor. New York and London, 1961.

——*On the Sacraments of the Christian Faith*, tr. Roy J. Deferrari. Cambridge, Mass., 1951.

Hughes, Philip. *The Church in Crisis: A History of the General Councils, 325–1870*. Garden City, N. Y., 1961.

Hulme, William Henry. *The Middle-English Harrowing of Hell and Gospel of Nicodemus*. London: EETS, 1907.

Jackson, Kenneth. *Language and History in Early Britain: A Chronological Survey of the Brittonic Languages, First to Twelfth Century A.D.* Cambridge, Mass., 1953.

James, Montague Rhodes, ed. and tr. *The Apocryphal New Testament*. Oxford, 1924.

Jenner, Henry. "The Cornish Drama." 4 unpublished lectures, delivered at Exeter University, 1928, in the Nance Bequest, Royal Institution of Cornwall, Truro.

—— "The Easter Sepulchre and Its Uses, with Some Remarks on the Dramatic Element in Church Services," *Journal of the Royal Institution of Cornwall*, 20 (1915–1921): 314–339.

—— "The Fourteenth-Century Charter Endorsement, Brit. Mus. Add. Ch. 19491," *Journal of the Royal Institution of Cornwall*, 20 (1915–1921): 41–48.

—— *A Handbook of the Cornish Language*. London, 1904.

—— "The Sources of the Cornish Drama." An unpublished lecture delivered at Exeter University [1932?], in the Nance Bequest, Royal Institution of Cornwall, Truro.

—— and Thomas Taylor. "The Legend of the Church of the Holy Cross in Cornwall," *Journal of the Royal Institution of Cornwall*, 20 (1915–1921): 295–309.

Jones, Leslie W. "The Influence of Cassiodorus on Mediaeval Culture," *Speculum*, 20 (1945): 433–442.

Jungmann, Joseph A. *The Mass of the Roman Rite: Its Origins and Development*, tr. Francis A. Brunner. 2 vols. New York and elsewhere, 1951–1955.

Kampers, Franz. *Mittelalterliche Sagen vom Paradiese und vom Holze des Kreuzes Christi in ihren vornehmsten Quellen und in ihren hervorstechendsten Typen.* Cologne, 1897.

Katzenellenbogen, Adolf. *The Sculptural Programs of Chartres Cathedral.* Baltimore, 1959.

Ker, N. R. "An Eleventh-Century Old English Legend of the Cross before Christ," *Medium Aevum,* 9 (1940): 84–85.

Kitzinger, Ernst. *Early Medieval Art in the British Museum.* 2nd ed. London, 1960.

Knowles, David. *The Religious Orders in England.* 3 vols. Cambridge, Eng., 1950–59.

Köhler, Reinhold. *Kleinere Schriften.* 3 vols. Weimar and Berlin, 1898–1900.

Kolve, V. A. *The Play Called Corpus Christi.* Stanford, Calif., 1966.

Krapp, George Philip, and Elliott Van Kirk Dobbie, edd. *The Anglo-Saxon Poetic Records: The Exeter Book.* New York, 1936.

Kretzmann, Paul Edward. *The Liturgical Element in the Earliest Forms of the Medieval Drama, with Special Reference to the English and German Plays.* Minneapolis: The University of Minnesota Studies in Language and Literature, vol. IV, 1916.

Künstle, Karl. *Ikonographie der Christlichen Kunst.* 2 vols. Freiburg, 1928.

Lach-Szyrma, W. S. *A Church History of Cornwall and of the Diocese of Truro.* London and elsewhere, n.d.

Ladner, Gerhart B. *The Idea of Reform: Its Impact on Christian Thought and Action in the Age of the Fathers.* Cambridge, Mass., 1959.

Lagarde, André [Joseph Turmel]. *The Latin Church in the Middle Ages,* tr. Archibald Alexander. New York, 1915.

Laistner, M. L. W. "Antiochene Exegesis in Western Europe during the Middle Ages," *Harvard Theological Review,* 40 (1947): 19–31.

Lanyon-Orgill, P. A. "The Cornish Drama," *The Cornish Review,* Spring 1949, pp. 38–42.

Laut, Stephen Joseph. "Drama Illustrating Dogma: A Study of the York Cycle." Doctoral dissertation, The University of North Carolina, 1960.

Lawson, John. *A Theological and Historical Introduction to the Apostolic Fathers.* New York, 1961.

Le Braz, Anatole. *Le Théâtre celtique,* Paris, n.d.

Leff, Gordon. "The Changing Pattern of Thought in the Earlier Fourteenth Century," *Bulletin of the John Rylands Library,* 43 (1960–1961): 354–372.

Legg, J. Wickham, ed. *The Sarum Missal, Edited from Three Early Manuscripts.* Oxford, 1916.

Loomis, Roger S., and Gustave Cohen. "Were There Theatres in the Twelfth and Thirteenth Centuries?" *Speculum,* 20 (1945): 92–98.

Loth, Joseph. *Introduction au Livre noir de Carmarthen et aux vieux poèmes gallois: la métrique galloise depuis les plus anciens textes jusqu' à nos jours.* 3 vols. Paris: Cours de littérature celtique, vols. IX–XI, 1900–1902.

Lubac, Henri de. *Exégèse médiévale: les quatre sens de l' Ecriture.* 2 vols. Paris, 1959.

Luddy, Ailbe J., ed. and tr. *The Case of Peter Abelard.* Dublin, 1947.

—— *Life and Teaching of St. Bernard.* Dublin, 1927.

Lundberg, Per. *La Typologie baptismale dans l'ancienne église.* Leipzig and Uppsala: *Acta Seminarii Neotestamentici Upsaliensis* (X), 1942.

Lynch, William F. *Christ and Apollo: the Dimensions of the Literary Imagination.* New York, 1960.

McCulloch, J. A. *The Religion of the Ancient Celts.* Edinburgh, 1911.

McIntyre, John. *Saint Anselm and His Critics: A Reinterpretation of the 'Cur Deus Homo'.* Edinburgh, 1954.

Maclean, Magnus. *The Literature of the Celts: Its History and Romance.* Glasgow and Dublin, 1902.

McNeir, Waldo F. "The Corpus Christi Passion Plays as Dramatic Art," *Studies in Philology,* 48 (1951): 601–628.

Mâle, Emile. *L'Art religieux de la fin du moyen âge en France.* 3rd ed. Paris, 1925.

—— *L'Art religieux du XIIe siècle en France.* 5th ed. Paris, 1947.

—— *L'Art religieux du XIIIe siècle en France.* 8th ed. Paris, 1948.

Marbach, Carolus [Karl], ed. *Carmina scripturarum.* Strasbourg, 1907.

Markus, R. A. "Presuppositions of the Typological Approach to Scripture," *Church Quarterly Review,* 158 (1957): 442–451.

Marshall, Mary H. *"Theatre* in the Middle Ages: Evidence from Dictionaries and Glosses," *Symposium,* 4 (1950): 1–39.

Meyer, Wilhelm. "Die Geschichte des Kreuzholzes vor Christus," *Abhandlungen der philosophisch-philologischen Classe der königlich bayerischen Akademie der Wissenschaften,* vol. XVI (Munich, 1882), pt. ii, pp. 101–166.

Migne, J. P., ed. *Patrologiae Cursus Completus. Series Latina [PL],* 221 vols. (Paris, 1844–1864); Series Graeca *[PG],* 162 vols. (Paris, 1857–1912).

Milburn, R. L. P. *Early Christian Interpretations of History.* New York, 1954.

Mirk, John. *Mirk's Festial: A Collection of Homilies,* ed. Theodor Erbe. London: EETS, 1905.

Morris, Richard, ed. *Cursor Mundi.* 7 vols. London: EETS, 1874–1878.

———— ed. *Legends of the Holy Rood; Symbols of the Passion and Cross Poems.* London: EETS, 1871.

Mussafia, Adolfo. "Sulla leggenda del legno della Croce," *Sitzungsberichte der philosophisch-historischen Classe der kaiserlichen Akademie der Wissenschaften,* 63 (1869): 165–216.

Nance, R. Morton. "Cornish Miracle-Play Manuscripts." An unpublished lecture, read at a meeting of the Royal Institution of Cornwall (1941), in the Nance Bequest, Royal Institution of Cornwall, Truro.

———— "Corrections and Notes to Norris' *Ordinalia.*" An unpublished manuscript in the Nance Bequest, Royal Institution of Cornwall, Truro.

———— *A New Cornish-English Dictionary.* St. Ives, Eng., 1938; and rev. ed., *A Cornish-English Dictionary.* Marazion, Eng., 1955.

———— ed. and tr. "Pascon Agan Arluth," *Kernow* (April 1934–March 1936).

———— "The Plen an Gwary or Cornish Playing-Place," *Journal of the Royal Institution of Cornwall,* 24 (1935): 190–211.

———— and A. S. D. Smith, edd. and trs. *The Ordinalia.* An unpublished manuscript in the Nance Bequest, Royal Institution of Cornwall, Truro.

Napier, Arthur S. *History of the Holy Rood-tree.* London: EETS, 1894.

Neale, J. M. *Essays on Liturgiology and Church History.* 2nd ed. London, 1867.

———— and Benjamin Webb, trs. *The Symbolism of Churches and Church Ornaments: A Translation of the First Book of the Rationale Divinorum Officiorum, Written by William Durandus, Sometime Bishop of Mende.* Leeds, 1843.

Norris, Edwin, ed. and tr. *The Ancient Cornish Drama.* 2 vols. Oxford, 1859.

Oakeshott, Walter. *The Sequence of English Medieval Art, Illustrated Chiefly from Illuminated MSS, 650–1450.* London, 1950.

Oberman, Heiko Augustinus. *The Harvest of Medieval Theology: Gabriel Biel and Late Medieval Nominalism.* Cambridge, Mass., 1963.

Owst, G. R. *Literature and Pulpit in Medieval England.* 2nd ed. New York, 1961.

———— *Preaching in Medieval England.* Cambridge, Eng., 1926.

Pantin, W. A. *The English Church in the Fourteenth Century.* Cambridge, Eng., 1955.

Parker, John, tr. *The Works of Dionysius the Areopagite.* 2 vols. London and Oxford, 1899.

Parry, John J. "The Revival of Cornish: An Dasserghyans Kernewek," *PMLA,* 61 (1946): 258–268.

Passmore, T. H., ed. and tr. *The Sacred Vestments: An English Rendering of the Third Book of the 'Rationale Divinorum Officiorum' of Durandus, Bishop of Mende.* London, 1899.

Patrologia Cursus Completus. See J. P. Migne.

Patterson, F. A. *The Middle English Penitential Lyric.* New York: Columbia University Studies in English, 1911.

Peebles, Bernard M. "Fortunatus, Poet of the Holy Cross," *American Church Monthly,* 38 (September 1935): 152–166.

Peebles, Rose Jeffries. "The Dry Tree: Symbol of Death," in Christabel Fiske, ed., *Vassar Mediaeval Studies* (New Haven, 1923), 59–79.

———— *The Legend of Longinus in Ecclesiastical Tradition and in English Literature, and Its Connection with the Grail.* Baltimore, 1911.

Pépin, Jean. *Mythe et allégorie.* Paris, 1958.

Peter, Thurstan C. *The History of Glasney Collegiate Church, Cornwall.* Camborne, Eng., 1903.

———— *The Old Cornish Drama.* London, 1906.

[*Piers Plowman.*] *The Vision of William Concerning Piers the Plowman, in Three Parallel Texts, together with Richard the Redeless, by William Langland,* ed. Walter W. Skeat. 2 vols. Oxford, 1886.

Pindar, Peter [John Wolcot]. *Lyric Odes for the Year 1785.* London, 1786.

Pollard, A. W., ed. *English Miracle Plays, Moralities, and Interludes.* 8th ed. Oxford, 1954.

Polwhele, Richard. *The Language, Literature, and Literary Characters of Cornwall: With Illustrations from Devonshire.* London, 1806.

Poole, Austin Lane, ed. *Medieval England.* Rev. ed. 2 vols. Oxford, 1958.

Prosser, Eleanor. *Drama and Religion in the English Mystery Plays: A Re-evaluation.* Stanford, Calif., 1961.

Puech, Henri-Charles. "Origène et l'exégèse trinitaire du Psaume 50. 12–14," *Aux sources de la tradition chrétienne: Mélanges offerts à M. Maurice Goguel* (Neufchatel and Paris, 1950), pp. 180–194.

Quinn, Esther Casier. *The Quest of Seth for the Oil of Life.* Chicago, 1962.

Raby, F. J. E. *A History of Christian-Latin Poetry from the Beginnings to the Close of the Middle Ages.* 2nd ed. Oxford, 1953.

Ragusa, Isa, ed. and tr., and Rosalie B. Green, ed. *Meditations on the Life of Christ: An Illustrated Manuscript of the Fourteenth Century; Paris, Bibliothèque Nationale, MS. ITAL. 115.* Princeton, 1961.

Rahner, Hugo. *Greek Myths and Christian Mystery,* tr. Brian Battershaw. London, 1963.

Rashdall, Hastings. *The Idea of Atonement in Christian Theology.* London, 1919.

Réau, Louis. *Iconographie de l'art chrétien.* 3 vols. Paris, 1955–1959.

Reese, Gustave. *Music in the Middle Ages.* New York, 1940.

Ringbom, Lars-Ivar. *Paradisus Terrestris: Myt, Bild och Verklighet.* Helsingfors, 1958.

Rivière, Jean. *Le Dogme de la rédemption après saint Augustin.* Paris, 1930.

———— "Le Dogme de la Rédemption au XIIe siècle d'après les dernières publications," *Revue du Moyen Age latin,* 2 (1946): 101–112, 219–230.

———— *Le Dogme de la rédemption au début du moyen âge.* Paris, 1934.

———— *Le Dogme de la rédemption chez saint Augustin.* 3rd ed. Paris, 1933.

———— *Le Dogme de la rédemption: Essai d'étude historique.* Paris, 1905.

———— *Le Dogme de la rédemption: Etudes critiques et documents.* Louvain, 1931.

Robbins, Rossell Hope, and John L. Cutler. *Supplement to the Index of Middle English Verse.* Lexington, Ken., 1965.

Rohault de Fleury, Ch[arles]. *Mémoire sur les Instruments de la Passion de N.-S. J.-C.* Paris, 1870.

Roques, René, ed. and tr. *Anselme de Cantorbéry: Pourquoi Dieu s'est fait homme.* Paris, 1963.

Rowse, A. L. *Tudor Cornwall: Portrait of a Society.* London, 1941.

Rufinus, Tyrannius. *A Commentary on the Apostles' Creed,* tr. J. N. D. Kelly. Westminster, Md., and London, 1955.

Russell, G. H. "Vernacular Instruction of the Laity in the Later Middle Ages in England: Some Texts and Notes," *The Journal of Religious History,* 2 (1962): 98–119.

Salter, F. M. *Mediaeval Drama in Chester.* Toronto, 1955.

Schoeps, H. J. *Paul: The Theology of the Apostle in the Light of Jewish Religious History,* tr. Harold Knight. Philadelphia, 1961.

———— "The Sacrifice of Isaac in Paul's Theology," *Journal of Biblical Literature,* 65 (1946): 385–392.

Sepet, M. C. A. *Les Prophètes du Christ: étude sur les origines du théâtre au moyen âge*. Paris, 1867–1868.

Sikes, J. G. *Peter Abailard*. Cambridge, Eng., 1932.

Smalley, Beryl. *English Friars and Antiquity in the Early Fourteenth Century*. Oxford, 1960.

────── *The Study of the Bible in the Middle Ages*. 2nd ed. Oxford, 1952.

Smart, James D. *The Interpretation of Scripture*. Philadelphia, 1961.

Southern, Richard. *The Medieval Theatre in the Round*. London, 1957.

Southern, R. W. *The Making of the Middle Ages*. New Haven, 1961.

────── *Saint Anselm and His Biographer*. Cambridge, Eng., 1963.

Spencer, M. Lyle. *Corpus Christi Pageants in England*. New York, 1911.

Steger, Hugo. *David, rex et propheta: König David als vorbildliche Verkörperung des Herrschers und Dichters im Mittelalter, nach Bilddarstellungen des achten bis zwölften Jahrhunderts*. Nuremburg, 1961.

Stokes, Whitley. "A Collation of Norris' *Ancient Cornish Drama*," *Archiv für celtische Lexikographie*, 1 (Halle, 1898): 161–174.

────── "Cornica," *Revue celtique*, 4 (1878–1881): 258–264.

────── ed. and tr. *Gwreans an Bys: the Creation of the World, a Cornish Mystery*. Berlin, 1863; London and Edinburgh, 1864.

────── ed. and tr. *The Life of St. Meriasek, Bishop and Confessor: A Cornish Drama*. London, 1872.

────── ed. and tr. "The Passion" (*Pascon Agan Arluth*), *Transactions of the Philological Society* (1860–1861), Appendix, pp. 1–100.

Suchier, Hermann. *Denkmäler Provenzalischer Literatur und Sprache*. Halle, 1883.

Taylor, Jerome. "The Dramatic Structure of the Middle English Corpus Christi, or Cycle, Plays," in Bernice Slote, ed., *Literature and Society* (Lincoln, Neb., 1964), pp. 175–186.

Taylor, Thomas. *The Celtic Christianity of Cornwall*. London and elsewhere, 1916.

Thomas, Charles. "The Society's 1962 Excavations: The Henge at Castilly, Lanivet," *Cornish Archaeology*, no. 3 (1964), pp. 3–14.

Turner, H. E. W. *The Patristic Doctrine of Redemption*. London, 1952.

Tuve, Rosemond. *A Reading of George Herbert*. Chicago, 1952.

Tyrer, John Walton. *Historical Survey of Holy Week: Its Services and Ceremonial*. London: Alcuin Club Collections, 1932.

Utley, Francis Lee. "The Prose *Salomon and Saturn* and the Tree Called Chy," *Mediaeval Studies*, 19 (1957): 55–78.

Vagaggini, Ciprian. *Theological Dimensions of the Liturgy*, tr. Leonard J. Doyle. Collegeville, Minn., 1959.

Warner, George F., and Julius P. Gilson. *Catalogue of Western MSS in the Old Royal and King's Collections.* 4 vols. London: British Museum, 1921.

Watson, Arthur. *The Early Iconography of the Tree of Jesse.* London, 1934.

Westra, M. Salvina, ed. *A Talkying of þe Loue of God.* The Hague, 1950.

Wickham, Glynne. *Early English Stages, 1300 to 1660.* 2 vols. London and New York, 1959–1963.

Williams, Arnold. *The Drama of Medieval England.* East Lansing, Mich., 1961.

Williams, George Huntston. "The Sacramental Presuppositions of Anselm's *Cur Deus Homo*," *Church History,* 26 (1957): 245–274.

Wilmart, André. *Analecta Reginensia: Extraits des manuscrits latins de la reine Christine conservés au Vatican.* Vatican City, 1933.

——— *Auteurs spirituels et textes dévots du moyen âge latin.* Paris, 1932.

Woolf, Rosemary. "Doctrinal Influences on *The Dream of the Rood*," *Medium Aevum,* 27 (1958): 137–153.

Wright, Jean Gray. *A Study of the Themes of the Resurrection in the Mediaeval French Drama.* Bryn Mawr, Pa., 1935.

Young, Karl. *The Drama of the Medieval Church.* 2 vols. Oxford, 1933.

——— *The Dramatic Associations of the Easter Sepulchre.* Madison: University of Wisconsin Studies in Language and Literature, vol. X, 1920.

Notes

1. Introduction

1. The *Ordinalia* was edited and translated by Edwin Norris in 1859 (*The Ancient Cornish Drama*, Oxford, 2 vols.), but this edition is now hard to come by and, although a remarkable scholarly achievement in its own right, is at present inadequate. Whitley Stokes published some corrections to this edition, in "A Collation of Norris' *Ancient Cornish Drama*," *Archiv für celtische Lexikographie*, 1 (Halle, 1898): 161–174. R. Morton Nance and A. S. D. Smith prepared an edition that combines a more accurate manuscript reading with a unified Cornish orthography and a smoother translation, but this edition languishes, for want of publication, in typescript at the County Museum of the Royal Institution of Cornwall, at Truro, among the papers of the Morton Nance Bequest. Phyllis Pier Harris has edited and translated the first part of the *Ordinalia* as a doctoral dissertation, "*Origo Mundi*, First Play of the Cornish Mystery Cycle, the *Ordinalia*: A New Edition" (University of Washington, 1964). Citations from the *Ordinalia* in my text are to Norris' edition, although I have consulted the Nance-Smith typescript and Mrs. Harris' dissertation. I have occasionally altered Norris' translation in order to provide a smoother and, in light of recent scholarship, more accurate text, but important differences of interpretation are noted.

2. For a discussion of this small corpus of Cornish literature, see Henry Jenner, *A Handbook of the Cornish Language* (London, 1904), pp. 24–46.

3. *Ancient Cornish Drama*, II, 508.

4. Paris, n.d., p. 101.

5. *Etudes d'histoire du théâtre en France au moyen-age et à la Renaissance* (Paris, 1956), pp. 385–386.

6. *English Religious Drama of the Middle Ages* (Oxford, 1955), p. 73.

7. Again with the Breton *Passion*, both Le Braz and Cohen concur in ascribing its origins to imitation, this time of French *mystères*.

But Cohen is more specific: "La scène des adieux de Jésus et de sa mère, le dialogue de Judas et de 'Désespérance', les noms des 'tyrans' décèlent assez l'imitation de *la Passion* d'Arnoul Greban ou même de celle de Jean Michel, qui, étant au plus tot de 1486, ne permet pas d'assigner à la Passion bretonne une date plus ancienne" (p. 388). See also Le Braz, *Le Théâtre celtique,* p. 251. For the date of the *Ordinalia,* see below.

8. In "The Cornish Drama," a series of four unpublished lectures given at Exeter University about 1928 and now deposited in the Morton Nance Bequest at the County Museum of the Royal Institution of Cornwall, p. 50.

9. See Frances A. Foster, ed., *The Northern Passion* (London: EETS, 1916), II, 101.

10. See Eleanor Prosser, *Drama and Religion in the English Mystery Plays* (Stanford, Calif., 1961), p. 169.

11. On the other hand, David C. Fowler interestingly if not persuasively has suggested that the author of the B-text of *Piers Plowman* knew and used at least part of the *Ordinalia,* "and that he had, therefore, in all probability, some knowledge of the Cornish language." The traffic moves in both directions. See *Piers the Plowman: Literary Relations of the A and B Texts* (Seattle, Wash., 1961), pp. 67–68.

12. *The Fyrst Boke of the Introduction of Knowledge,* ed. F. J. Furnivall (London: EETS, 1870), p. 123.

13. *The Survey of Cornwall,* ed. F. E. Halliday (London, 1953), p. 127. Carew's illustrious *Survey* was first published in 1602 and was dedicated to Sir Walter Raleigh. Dr. John Ken(n)all, who died in 1592, had the living of several Cornish churches, and was a secular chaplain, archdeacon of Rochester and Oxford, and Canon of Exeter. See Joseph Foster, *Alumni Oxonienses: The Members of the University of Oxford, 1500–1714,* 4 vols. (London, 1891–92).

14. "Antiquities Cornubritannic," etc., a manuscript in the library of the County Museum of the Royal Institution of Cornwall.

15. Both the letter and the verses are printed by Richard Polwhele, *The Language, Literature, and Literary Characters, of Cornwall: With Illustrations from Devonshire* (London, 1806), p. 19, in his discussion of the last traces of the language. The verse is from Ode XXI, "To Myself," in *Lyric Odes for the Year 1785* (London, 1786), by Peter Pindar [John Wolcot].

16. In Davies Gilbert, *The Parochial History of Cornwall* (London, 1838), IV, 206.

17. See, for example, A. L. Rowse, *Tudor Cornwall* (London, 1941), p. 23.

18. See Rowse, *Tudor Cornwall,* p. 23; and L. E. Elliott-Binns, *Medieval Cornwall* (London, 1955), p. 404.

19. An early and very inaccurate edition is that of Davies Gilbert, *The Creation of the World, With Noah's Flood,* based on a translation by John Keigwyn (London, 1827). A later and better edition is Whitley Stokes, *Gwreans an Bys: the Creation of the World, a Cornish Mystery* (Berlin, 1863; London and Edinburgh, 1864). Most recently *Gwryans an Bys* has appeared, ed. and tr. R. Morton Nance and A. S. D. Smith (n.d.), bound but in mimeograph form.

20. In Gilbert, *Parochial History,* IV, 204–205. Gilbert wrongly takes *Guirremears* to mean "speeches great."

21. This description of the manuscript is considerably indebted to notes jotted down by R. Morton Nance and preserved among the papers of the Nance Bequest in the County Museum of the Royal Institution of Cornwall. Usually by means of photostats, Nance devoted a great deal of labor to ascertaining the readings emended by scribal corrections, and he notes that though "in many places these are seen quite clearly . . . in others they are quite lost."

22. See E. K. Chambers, *The Mediaeval Stage* (Oxford, 1903), II, 433. Nance, in his notes, tentatively suggests the latter half of the fifteenth century. Malcolm Parkes, who has kindly looked into the manuscript at my request, is inclined to agree with the later dating, and thinks it may be as late as 1500.

23. *Ancient Cornish Drama,* II, 473–514. The religious foundation is discussed in Thurstan C. Peter, *The History of Glasney Collegiate Church, Cornwall* (Camborne, Eng., 1903).

24. *Survey of Cornwall,* p. 144.

25. "The Society's 1962 Excavations: The Henge at Castilly, Lanivet," *Cornish Archaeology,* no. 3 (1964), pp. 10–12. R. Morton Nance discusses the western "rounds" in "The Plen an Gwary or Cornish Playing-Place," *Journal of the Royal Institution of Cornwall,* 24 (1935): 190–211. An interesting though rather more fanciful treatment than Nance's is Richard Southern, *The Medieval Theatre in the Round* (London, 1957). Since other sports and spectacles, such as wrestling, have long been popular in Cornwall and have used these "rounds," the suggestion by P. A. Lanyon-Orgill, "The Cornish Drama," *The Cornish Review,* Spring 1949, pp. 38–42, that the "amphitheatres [were] especially constructed for the purpose" of presenting the dramas, seems unwarranted.

26. Chambers, while frowning dubiously at E. H. Pedler's opinion —set down in an Appendix to Norris' *Ancient Cornish Drama* (II, 506) —that the *Ordinalia* could be dated at the close of the thirteenth century, was himself rather vague about the problem, saying only that it is "not earlier in date than the fourteenth century" (*Mediaeval Stage,* II, 433). Alfred Harbage, in *Annals of English Drama, 975–1700,* rev. S. Schoenbaum (London and Philadelphia, 1964), without comment indicates the distributory limits of the drama as about 1300–1325.

27. "The Date of the Cornish *Ordinalia*," *Mediaeval Studies,* 23 (1961): 91–125. See especially p. 125.

28. Fowler, "Date," pp. 103–104.

29. Norris, *Ancient Cornish Drama,* II, 506.

30. Fowler, "Date," p. 104.

31. *Ibid.,* pp. 104–113.

32. *Ibid.,* pp. 120–124.

33. *Handbook,* p. 11.

34. *Ancient Cornish Drama,* II

35. See the excellent discussion of the *Old Cornish Vocabulary,* along with other examples of Old Cornish, in Kenneth Jackson, *Language and History in Early Britain* (Cambridge, Mass., 1953), pp. 59–62. The vocabulary has been edited and annotated by Eugene Van Tassel Graves, "The Old Cornish Vocabulary," as a doctoral dissertation (Columbia University, 1962).

36. *Gwreans an Bys,* and *The Life of Saint Meriasek, Bishop and Confessor: a Cornish Drama* (London, 1872); "The Passion" (*Pascon Agan Arluth*), an appendix to *Transactions of the Philological Society,* 1860–61, pp. 1–100.

37. St. Ives, Eng., 1938. The work has been revised and published, unfortunately with a great deal of helpful material omitted, as *A Cornish-English Dictionary* (Marazion, Eng., 1955). These twentieth century scholars and their work represent at its best the revival of interest in the language described at length by John J. Parry, "The Revival of Cornish: An Dasserghyans Kernewek," *PMLA,* 61 (1946): 258–268.

38. Professor Dunn has pointed out to me that such phrases are common to Celtic poetry and are called *geiriau llanw* (empty words) by the Welsh.

39. Indeed, the list of *dramatis personae* at the end of each day's play includes a set of numbers that apparently indicates not how many speeches but how many stanzas are spoken by each character.

40. *Ancient Cornish Drama,* II, 447.

41. See Joseph Loth, *Introduction au Livre noir de Carmarthen et aux vieux poèmes gallois: la métrique galloise depuis les plus anciens textes jusqu'à nos jours* (Paris: Cours de littérature celtique, 1900–1902), II, 204–216.

42. Nance, in an interesting unpublished note left among his papers on the *Ordinalia* now in the Nance Bequest, suggests that the poetry may have been "more nearly chanted than spoken." He points out that in the manuscript the expected breaks between words are frequently omitted so as to give "the artificial spacing of a line," which may emphasize "its scansion rather than its sense." This theory clearly aims to resolve both orthographic peculiarities in the manuscript and the apparent metrical monotony of the verse, but it is worth more as an index to a scholar's bewilderment than as an authoritative prosodic judgment.

43. See M. Lyle Spencer, *Corpus Christi Pageants in England* (New York, 1911), p. 8; Chambers, *Mediaeval Stage,* II, 94, 138; Hermann Deimling, ed., *The Chester Plays* (London: EETS, 1893), I, 1; and Robert Fitch, ed., *Norwich Pageants: The Grocers' Plays* (Norwich, 1856), pp. 3, 8.

44. In Nance, "The Plen an Gwary," pp. 190–211.

45. Whitley Stokes, ed., *The Life of Saint Meriasek,* following line 1865. Here and elsewhere in my transcriptions, superior letters are brought down.

46. *Ancient Cornish Drama,* II, 456.

47. Karl Young, *The Drama of the Medieval Church* (Oxford, 1933), II, 410.

48. Chambers, *Mediaeval Stage,* II, 68f, suggested that the festival of Corpus Christi, a love of processions, and increasing secularization were responsible for moving the drama out of the church and its liturgical setting, and he consequently regarded the development of the cycles as a long process of secularization. Craig, *English Religious Drama,* pp. 73 and 88f, thinks rather that the secularization was subsequent to the building of the cycles, behind which he sees the properly syncretistic impulses of the liturgical year and scriptural history. More sharply at variance with the traditional ideas is Glynne Wickham, *Early English Stages, 1300 to 1600,* I (London and New York, 1959), who suggests that the drama may not only have developed but may also have continued to flourish under the protection and direction of the clergy, and that "secularization" is a term misapplied to its growth (see esp. pp. 124f). An example of the general speculation endemic to this subject is Arnold Williams, *The Drama of Medieval England* (Michigan State University, East Lansing, Mich., 1961), pp. 38f. G. R. Owst suggests that "it was *popular preaching* . . . that brought about the 'secularization' of the drama. Every feature characteristic of this new presentation of the plays is familiar to us already in the methods of open-air preaching inaugurated by the friars." *Literature and Pulpit in Medieval England* (New York, 1961), p. 478.

49. Harold Ehrensperger, *Religious Drama: Ends and Means* (New York, 1962), p. 22.

50. Eleanor Prosser, *Drama and Religion,* p. 177.

51. For a rare instance of swift-moving dialogue, see the exchanges between the jailor and his servant (*PC* 2239–2336); the comic incident of the leprous smith is an example of rather well-turned wit; the apostle Thomas emerges as a character whose disbelief and self-recrimination doubtless elicit the sympathy and interest of the spectator.

52. See, for example, Foster, ed., *The Northern Passion,* pp. 81–101; the same author's edition of *A Stanzaic Life of Christ* (London: EETS, 1926), pp. xxviii–xlii; and Grace Frank, "Vernacular Sources and an Old French Passion Play," *Modern Language Notes,* 35 (1920): 257–269.

53. See, for example, David Knowles, *The Religious Orders in England* (Cambridge, Eng., 1950), esp. I, ix f.

54. David Knowles, in Austin Lane Poole, ed., *Medieval England* (Oxford, 1958), II, 410. Beryl Smalley, in *English Friars and Antiquity in the Early Fourteenth Century* (Oxford, 1960), has added weight to this generalization by her thorough and lucid studies of a number of these mendicants. Miss Smalley remarks that "all the friars are moralists, responding to public demand for new and striking exempla . . . The friars' blend of fact and fancy influenced English literature more than their scholarship did" (pp. 306–307).

55. See Philip Hughes, *The Church in Crisis* (New York, 1960), pp. 214–221.

56. See, for example, W. A. Pantin, *The English Church in the Fourteenth Century* (Cambridge, Eng., 1955), p. 187, and the evidence set down by G. H. Russell, "Vernacular Instruction of the Laity in the Later Middle Ages in England: Some Texts and Notes," *The Journal of Religious History,* 2 (1962): 98–119.

57. *Mediaeval Stage,* II, 77–78n. Italics mine. See also the discussion of this note by Glynne Wickham, *Early English Stages,* pp. 141f.

2. The Ordinalia and the Bible

1. John Donne, *Devotions upon Emergent Occasions,* ed. John Sparrow (Cambridge, Eng., 1923), p. 113.

2. H. H. Glunz, *History of the Vulgate in England from Alcuin to Roger Bacon* (Cambridge, Eng., 1933), p. 99. A particularly valuable discussion of this general problem is Oscar Cullman, *Christ and Time: the Primitive Christian Conception of Time and History,* 3rd ed., tr. Floyd V. Filson (London, 1962).

3. The great pioneer in elucidating this attitude was Emile Mâle. See particularly *L'Art religieux du XIIe siècle en France,* 5th ed. (Paris, 1947); *L'Art religieux du XIIIe siècle en France,* 8th ed. (Paris, 1948); *L'Art religieux de la fin du moyen âge en France,* 3rd ed. (Paris, 1925), esp. pp. 35–84, for the relationship between art and the drama. Mention must be made, too, of the very helpful and extensive study by Louis Réau, *Iconographie de l'art chrétien,* 3 vols. (Paris, 1955–1959).

4. *Vita Sanctorum Abbatum Monasterii in Uyrmutha et Gyruum,* in J. E. King, ed., *Opera Historica* (Cambridge, Mass., and London: Loeb Classical Library, 1954), II, 404–406.

5. M. L. W. Laistner, "Antiochene Exegesis in Western Europe during the Middle Ages," *Harvard Theological Review,* 40 (1947): 31.

6. See, for example, the summary—not itself disinterested—of some recent trends in William F. Lynch, *Christ and Apollo: the Dimensions of the Literary Imagination* (New York, 1960), pp. 253–267. The most satisfactory study of the subject, combining a cogent interpretive approach with a mass of materials drawn from the fathers, is Henri de Lubac, *Exégèse médiévale: les quatre sens de l'Ecriture,* 2 vols. (Paris, 1959), my debt to which is readily apparent in these pages.

7. Summarizing Paul's use of typology as an exegetical approach, Leonhard Goppelt argues that "Die Typologie zeigt nicht nur das Wesen des Neuen gegenüber dem Alten, sondern auch, dass es gerade und nur auf diesem heilsgeschichtlichen Grunde steht. Diese Typologie ist gewiss bei Paulus exegetisch unterbaut und in theologischer Reflexion ausgestaltet, aber sie ist auch bei ihm keine systematische Schriftdeutung, sondern eine pneumatische Betrachtungsweise." (Typology not only shows the essence of the new in relation to the old, but also shows that the essence rests exactly and solely on this basis of salvation-history. In Paul this typology is certainly established exegetically and shaped in theological reflection, yet in his thought it is no systematic means of scriptural interpretation, but a spiritual method of contemplation.) *Typos: Die typologische Deutung des Alten Testaments im Neuen. Beiträge zur Förderung christlicher Theologie,* II, 43 (Gütersloh, Germ., 1939), p. 183. See also H. J. Schoeps, *Paul: the Theology of the Apostle in the Light of Jewish Religious History,* tr. Harold Knight (Philadelphia, 1961), pp. 229–235, and R. A. Markus, "Presuppositions of the Typological Approach to Scripture," *Church Quarterly Review,* 158 (1957): 442–451.

8. "Jerusalem is understood historically of that earthly city whither pilgrims journey; allegorically, of the Church Militant; tropologically, of every faithful soul; anagogically, of the celestial Jerusalem, which is our Country." Durandus goes on to say that "more examples may be seen in the lessons for Holy Saturday." *The Symbolism of Churches and Church Ornaments: A Translation of the First Book of the Rationale Divinorum Officiorum,* tr. John Mason Neale and Benjamin Webb (Leeds, 1843), p. 11.

9. PL, CXIII, 29. See Lubac, *Exégèse médiévale,* II, 417.

10. The corollary, of course, is that the medieval cycles were in fact history plays, or plays that treated history, however general and religious. E. Catherine Dunn makes this point in "The Medieval 'Cycle' as History Play: an Approach to the Wakefield Plays," *Studies in the Renaissance*, 7 (1960): 76–89. For a very general background to the problem of history in Christian thought, see R. L. P. Milburn, *Early Christian Interpretations of History* (New York, 1954), although the book concerns itself more particularly with historiography.

11. "Typologische Motive in der mittelalterlichen Literatur," *Schriften und Vorträge des Petrarca-Instituts Köln*, 2 (Krefeld, Germ., 1953): 13.

12. Jean Daniélou, *From Shadows to Reality: Studies in the Biblical Typology of the Fathers*, tr. Wulstan Hibberd (Westminster, Md., 1960), p. 31.

13. *Didascalion*, tr. Jerome Taylor (New York and London, 1961), V, ii (p. 121).

14. *Exégèse médiévale*, I, 198–199.

15. "Symbolism in Medieval Literature," *Modern Philology*, 56 (1958): 74n.

16. Auerbach suggests that the "medieval Christian drama . . . opens its arms invitingly to receive the simple and untutored and to lead them from the concrete, the everyday, to the hidden and the true." *Mimesis: the Representation of Reality in Western Literature*, tr. Willard R. Trask (Princeton, 1953), p. 155.

17. *In Ezekiel*, I, vi, 15 (*PL*, LXXVI, 835).

18. Lubac notes that this symbolism was popular, and was used, for example, by Rabanus Maurus, Wolberon, Odo of Cluny, Honorius, Ailred, and others. *Exégèse médiévale*, I, 351.

19. *Sermo de Tentatione Abrahae a Deo, PL* XXXVIII, 30–31.

20. *Treatise of the Holy Spirit* (*PG*, XXXII, 121C), quoted and tr. by Daniélou, *Shadows to Reality*, p. 188.

21. See M. D. Chenu, "Théologie symbolique et exégèse scolastique aux XIIe–XIIIe siècles," *Mélanges Joseph de Ghellinck* (Gembloux, Belg., 1951), II, 520.

22. Erich Auerbach notes that "beide Pole einer typologischen Figur bewahren ihre historisch reale Konkretheit; der typologische Sinn zerstört nicht den wörtlich historischen Sinn des prophetischen Ereignisses, und auch die auf diese Weise figurierte Erfüllung ist stets ein als wirklich geschehend erwartetes Ereignis, nicht eine Abstraktion." (Both poles of a typological figure preserve their historical reality; the typological sense does not destroy the literal-historical sense of the prophetic event, and at the same time the fulfillment that is thus prefigured is always an event that is awaited as if really happening, and not an abstraction.) "Typologische Motive," pp. 8–9.

23. Glunz, for example, remarks that "it was the characteristic mark of biblical studies in the school of Alcuin and his successors (and, we may venture to generalise, of all scholasticism) that [the Bible] . . . was thought of as composed of a duality of word and sense, of outward text and inward meaning. The text was, as it were, a mask rather hiding the true meaning from the inquiring student than revealing it." *Vulgate,* pp. 84–85.

24. Moses was understandably a popular and familiar type of Christ. For example, British Museum MS. Harleian 1828 begins with a description of contents, "Moses et Aaron Sive Typi et Umbrae Domini Nostri Jesu Christi, in Veteri velati, in Novo Foedere revelati." (Moses and Aaron, or Types and Shadows of Our Lord Jesus Christ, Concealed in the Old Covenant and Revealed in the New.)

25. Unpublished lectures on The Cornish Drama, p. 73.

26. Réau, *Iconographie,* I, 198.

27. See Réau, I, 210–212, and Lubac, *Exégèse médiévale,* I, 339.

28. According to this scheme, "Le Christ vient donc ravir au diable cette Eglise qu'il tenait en un mariage illégitime, et par le seul acte de son sacrifice il tue le diable et célèbre ses noces avec son Eglise." (Christ came to wrest this Church from the devil who clung to it in an unlawful marriage, and by the single act of his sacrifice he slays the devil and celebrates his marriage with his Church.) Lubac suggests that this attitude is indicative of an insistent and assiduous application of typological consistency as found, for example, in Remigius of Auxerre's statement that "David ubique Christum significat" (David everywhere signifies Christ). *Exégèse médiévale,* II, 463.

29. A very general survey of the development of typological interpretation is in Raymond Edward Brown, *The 'Sensus Plenior' of Sacred Scripture* (Baltimore, 1955), pp. 29–62. See also Robert M. Grant, *A Short History of the Interpretation of the Bible* (New York, 1963).

30. Henri-Charles Puech, "Origène et l'exégèse trinitaire du Psaume 50. 12–14," *Aux sources de la tradition chrétienne: Mélanges offerts a M. Maurice Goguel* (Neufchatel and Paris, 1950), pp. 180–194.

31. Lucien Delporte, "Les Principes de la typologie biblique et les éléments figuratifs du Sacrifice de l'Expiation," *Ephemerides Theologicae Lovanienses,* 3 (1926): 313.

32. Daniélou, *Shadows to Reality,* p. 92.

33. Beryl Smalley cites as an example of this view of creation, "both historical and symbolical," Hugh of St. Victor's treatment of the days of creation, for he discusses their several mystical significations. *The Study of the Bible in the Middle Ages* (Oxford, 1952), p. 90.

34. For a discussion of the historical roots of this idea, and of

its exegetical implications, see Daniélou, *Shadows to Reality,* esp. pp. 11–21. The paradox of the *felix culpa* is a particular favorite among medieval writers.

35. See also 1 Corinthians 15:22, 15:45f.

36. "Hymn to God, My God, In My Sickness," lines 21–23. The "one place" was thought to be the center of the world.

37. This idea is briefly traced in Rheinhold Köhler, *Kleinere Schriften* (Weimar and Berlin, 1898–1900), II, 7–12. The typological connection is made explicit by the writer of the curious *Allegoriarum* in British Museum Royal MS. 4. D. VII—allegedly Peter Comestor but possibly Hugh of St. Victor, according to George F. Warner and Julius P. Gilson, *Catalogue of Western MSS. in the Old Royal and King's Collections* (London, 1921), I, 90—when he observes that "terra de qua primus homo factus est significat virginem . . . Virgo terra est virgo Maria" (The earth from which the first man was made signifies a virgin . . . The virgin land is [represents] the Virgin Mary) (III, *De primo homine*), an elaboration of the correspondence between Adam and Christ.

38. In passing, it seems worthwhile to remark Jenner's observation that "in the story of the marvellous ship in the Galahad Quest the Fate of Cain and Abel, with the tithe detail, is told almost exactly as in the Cornish drama. The 'Queste del Saint Graal' is about 200 years older than the drama and was not an unlikely book for the canon of Glasney College who wrote the latter to have read." "The Sources of the Cornish Drama," an unpublished lecture delivered at Exeter University [1932?], now in the Nance Bequest, p. 21.

39. See the stage direction following *OM* 1890; and *OM* 1931, 1944, 1956.

40. See, for example, James Hastings, ed., *A Dictionary of the Bible,* IV (New York, 1902), s.v. *Tabor.*

41. George Philip Krapp and Elliott Van Kirk Dobbie, edd., *The Anglo-Saxon Poetic Records: The Exeter Book* (New York, 1936), p. 163.

42. XV, xviii, tr. Marcus Dods (New York, 1950). Isidore of Seville (*PL,* LXXXIII, 101), Rabanus Maurus (*PL,* CXI, 32), Hugh of St. Victor (*PL,* CLXXV, 640), and Peter Comestor (*PL,* CXCVIII, 1080) are just a few of the commentators who echo Augustine.

43. Daniélou, *Shadows to Reality,* p. 69.

44. St. John Chrysostom (*PG,* XLVIII, 1037–1038), tr. Daniélou, *Shadows to Reality,* p. 101. Hugh of St. Victor observes, "Restat nunc ut videamus, quae sit arca Ecclesiae, vel ut expressius loquar, ipsa Ecclesia arca est, quam summus Noe, id est Dominus noster Jesus Christus, gubernator, et portus inter procellas hujus vitae regens per se ducit ad se" (It remains now that we may see what sort of ark the

Church may be; or, to speak more plainly, the Church herself *is* the ark, which the supreme Noah—that is, our Lord Jesus Christ—as steersman and as haven, piloting among the storms of this life, leads through himself to himself) (*PL*, CLXXVI, 629).

45. See, for example, Hugh of St. Victor [?], *Allegoriae in Vetus Testamentum*, I, xv (*PL*, CLXXV, 643).

46. See, for example, Tertullian, *De Baptismo*, in *PL*, I, 1209.

47. See *OM* 1209, 1227, 1233, 1250.

48. Tr. and quoted by Daniélou, *Shadows to Reality*, p. 129.

49. Daniélou has an able discussion of this subject, in *Shadows to Reality*, pp. 118–120. Particular mention may also be made of H. J. Schoeps, "The Sacrifice of Isaac in Paul's Theology," *Journal of Biblical Literature*, 65 (1946): 385–392: the point made here is that Paul's redemptive theology may look back to prechristian speculation on Isaac's sacrifice as a redemptive act in itself rather than as a test of Abraham's faith.

50. See Daniélou, *Shadows to Reality*, p. 224, who mentions particularly St. Gregory of Nyssa.

51. Daniélou notes that particularly in Eastern thought the Crossing of the Red Sea was regarded as a type of Christ's descent into Hell, but there seems to be no vestige of such a typology in the *Ordinalia*. *Shadows to Reality*, pp. 184–185.

52. See Daniélou, *Shadows to Reality*, pp. 232f.

3. The Legend of the Cross and the Interpretive Frame

1. The legend is taken from a commonplace book, British Museum Harl. MS. 2252, folios 50b–51b, by Henry Jenner and Thomas Taylor, "The Legend of the Church of the Holy Cross in Cornwall," *Journal of the Royal Institution of Cornwall*, 20 (1917–1921): 295–309. See also Charles Henderson, *The Ecclesiastical History of Cornwall* (Truro, Eng., 1962), pp. 187–188.

2. *Mémoire sur les instruments de la Passion de N.-S. J.-C.* (Paris, 1870), pp. 146–149. The most recent and comprehensive study of the various reported relics is A. Frolow, *La Relique de la vraie croix* (Paris, 1961).

3. The ceremony is discussed by Adrian Fortescue, *The Ceremonies of the Roman Rite Described*, 7th ed., rev. J. O'Connell (London, 1943), pp. 294–296; and by Louis Bouyer, *The Paschal Mystery*, tr. Mary Benoit (London, 1951), pp. 230–241. Its celebration in the Sarum rite is described in the rubrics of the *Missale ad Usum Insignis et Praeclarae Ecclesiae Sarum*, ed. Francis Henry Dickinson (Oxford and London, 1861–1883), cols. 328–331.

4. L. Duchesne, *Christian Worship,* tr. M. L. McClure, 4th ed. (London, 1912), pp. 510–511, 564–565.

5. Neil C. Brooks, *The Sepulchre of Christ in Art and Liturgy* (Urbana, Ill.: University of Illinois Studies in Language and Literature, 1921), p. 31, and Duchesne, *Christian Worship,* p. 248.

6. *Piers the Plowman,* p. 145.

7. See Brooks, *The Sepulchre of Christ,* p. 35; also Karl Young, *The Dramatic Associations of the Easter Sepulchre* (Madison, Wis.: University of Wisconsin Studies in Language and Literature, Vol. X, 1920), and *Drama of the Medieval Church,* I, 112–148.

8. The Latin text is printed by Wilhelm Meyer, "Die Geschichte des Kreuzholzes vor Christus," *Abhandlungen der philosophisch-philologischen Classe der königlich bayerischen Akademie der Wissenschaften,* Vol. XVI (Munich, 1882), pt. ii, pp. 101–166; by Hermann Suchier, *Denkmäler Provenzalischer Literatur und Sprache* (Halle, 1883), pp. 165–200; and by C. Horstmann, "Nachträge zu den Legenden," *Archiv für das Studium der neueren Sprachen und Litteraturen,* 79 (1887): 465–470.

9. Arthur S. Napier, *History of the Holy Rood-tree* (London: EETS, 1894), introduction, esp. p. xli. See N. R. Ker, "An Eleventh-Century Old English Legend of the Cross before Christ," *Medium Aevum,* 9 (1940): 84–85, for corroboration of part of Napier's hypothesis.

10. Esther Casier Quinn, *The Quest of Seth for the Oil of Life* (Chicago, 1962), esp. pp. 23f.

11. Other sources may have been used. The Pseudo-Clementine literature, for example, refers to Christ as the agent who "took the oil from the tree of life" and brought it to earth. See Edgar Hennecke, *Neutestamentliche Apokryphen* (Tübingen, 1924), p. 156.

12. Quoted from the translation of Latin text A by Montague Rhodes James, *The Apocryphal New Testament* (Oxford, 1924), p. 126.

13. See Quinn, *Quest,* p. 46. Miss Quinn is largely concerned with the cultural or archetypal origins of the oil and the wood as symbols (see p. 90), but such a problem is beyond the concern of the present study.

14. Cf. Latin text B, in James, *Apocryphal New Testament,* p. 128. In the Greek text, the archangel makes a point of asking Seth whether he seeks "the oil that raiseth up the sick, or . . . the tree that floweth with that oil" (p. 127).

15. *Apocrypha,* p. 127.

16. *Apocrypha,* pp. 137–138.

17. Quinn, for example, ingeniously suggests that the phrase may have arisen as a kind of felicitous pun on the two Greek words *elaios,* "olive-oil," and *eleos,* "mercy" (p. 27), and furthermore thinks that the idea belongs properly to the Jewish legend of Enoch's journey to paradise.

18. See Arthur Watson, *The Early Iconography of the Tree of Jesse* (London, 1934), pp. 52–54.

19. This excerpt, along with most of the others cited here, is printed by Meyer, "Geschichte," p. 115.

20. In addition to the manuscript versions of the Latin legend that Suchier draws on in his *Denkmäler Provenzalischer Literatur,* several others deserve mention. Among the most interesting is that in British Museum Royal MS. VI. E. 6, described as *"Omne Bonum,* a voluminous encyclopaedia of canon law, theology, and general information, compiled in the middle of the fourteenth century by Jacobus, an Englishman." Warner and Gilson, *Catalogue of Western MSS.,* I, 157. A text from the Worcester Cathedral Library has been printed by Betty Hill, "The Fifteenth-Century Prose *Legend of the Cross before Christ,"* *Medium Aevum,* 34 (1965): 203–222. In the Bodleian Library, MS. Douce 79 is a French version, and Canon MS. Ital. 280 is a rather careless fifteenth century version that has a number of crude illustrations along with the text. Bibliologically, the legend received perhaps its finest artistic treatment at the hands of the Dutch printer John Veldener who, in 1483, produced a versified Dutch translation illustrated with charming woodcuts. This work is reprinted in part by Thomas Frognall Dibdin, *Bibliotheca Spenceriana* (London, 1814–15), III, 348–377, and entirely by John Ashton, *The Legendary History of the Cross* (London, 1887), and J. Ph. Berjeau, *Geschiedenis van het heylighe Cruys; or, History of the Holy Cross* (London, 1863). In art, a remarkable window at St. Neot's in Cornwall depicts Seth placing the seeds under Adam's tongue—see J. P. Hedgeland, *A Description, Accompanied by Sixteen Coloured Plates, of the Splendid Decorations Recently Made to the Church of St. Neot in Cornwall* (London, 1830), p. 52; and of particular interest are the fourteenth century frescoes by Gaddi in the church of Santa Croce in Florence and the fifteenth century painting by Piero della Francesca in the choir of San Francesco at Arezzo, both of which deal with the legend of the cross.

21. Ed. Carl Horstmann (London: EETS, 1887), pp. 5–10.

22. Ed. Frances A. Foster (London: EETS, 1913), I, 134–167; and a supplement ed. Wilhelm Heuser and Frances A. Foster (London: EETS, 1930), pp. 31–34.

23. Ed. Theodor Erbe (London: EETS, 1905), pp. 142–143.

24. Ed. Richard Morris (London: EETS, 1874–78), I and II.

25. Ed. Carl Horstmann, *Sammlung altenglischer Legenden* (Heilbronn, Germ., 1878), pp. 131–138. For other examples in English not listed here, see Morris, *Legends of the Holy Rood.*

26. F. E. Halliday, ed. and tr., *The Legend of the Rood* (London, 1955), p. 49. Cf. Charles Mills Gayley, *Plays of Our Forefathers* (New York, 1907), p. 333. Napier suggested that the *Cursor Mundi* probably drew on an Old French version of the cross legend (*History of the Holy Rood-tree,* pp. xxiii–xxxi), but as Henry Jenner has pointed out, the Cornish version is much closer to the Latin than to the Old French poem, the *Passion des Jongleurs,* or to the material of *Cursor Mundi.* "Sources," p. 8.

27. For the tree, see Rose J. Peebles, "The Dry Tree: Symbol of Death," in Christabel Fiske, ed., *Vassar Mediaeval Studies* (New Haven, 1923), pp. 59–79. Quinn has a discussion of the tree and the child (*Quest,* pp. 112–125), although I am unconvinced by her argument "that the primary meaning of the great tree of Seth's vision is the great mother, bearing the baby who is to be the savior of the world" (p. 125). In addition to the examples from art cited by Peebles and Quinn, there is an example of what appears to be a phoenix in the tree from a fourth century mosaic of the Parousia in Ravenna, and a crucified Christ appears among the branches of a tree in a Salzburg miniature dated 1481. See Lars-Ivar Ringbom, *Paradisus Terrestris: Myt, Bild och Verklighet* (Helsingfors, 1958), pp. 55–57; and Hugo Rahner, *Greek Myths and Christian Mystery,* tr. Brian Battershaw (London, 1963), p. 42. Rosemond Tuve, in *A Reading of George Herbert* (Chicago, 1952), p. 83n, describes a swaddled babe in a tree among the sculpture of the choir in the cathedral at Toledo. The five-year-old child in the Perceval stories is a doubtful analogue, as E. Brugger points out in *The Illuminated Tree in Two Arthurian Romances* (New York, 1929).

28. Cited by Daniélou, *Shadows to Reality,* p. 35.

29. I owe this terminology to Gerhart Ladner, who remarks that the idea was particularly characteristic of Eastern theology. *The Idea of Reform* (Cambridge, Mass., 1959), p. 82n.

30. "For the Fathers," Daniélou remarks, "the mystical life was a return to Paradise." *Shadows to Reality,* p. 27.

31. See *Quest,* pp. 39–43.

32. Irenaeus, *Demonstration of the Apostolic Preaching,* quoted in Daniélou, *Shadows to Reality,* p. 45.

33. *Collationes in Hexaemeron,* ed. Ferdinandus Delorme (Florence, 1934), p. 7.

34. Although Quinn sees parallels to this motif in Celtic folk literature (p. 77), the dramatist could have had it directly from the legend.

35. Moses is particularly attracted by the sweet odor given off by the rods; this characteristic is reminiscent of the description of the cross in Venantius Fortunatus' great hymn, *Vexilla Regis:*

Fundis aroma cortice,
Vincis sapore nectare.

See Bernard M. Peebles, "Fortunatus, Poet of the Holy Cross," *The American Church Monthly*, 38 (September 1935): 152–166.

36. The Latin legend itself paraphrases Numbers 14:28–30: "Vivo ego, ait Dominus . . . Omnes, qui . . . murmurastis contra me, non intrabitis terram, per quam levavi manum meam, ut habitare vos facerem, praeter Caleb filium Jephone, et Josue filium Nun." (As I live, saith the Lord . . . All you that . . . have murmured against me, shall not enter into the land, over which I lifted up my hand to make you dwell therein, except Caleb the son of Jephone, and Josue [Joshua] the son of Nun. Douay version.) The story occurs also in Exodus 17:2–7.

37. Cf. Numbers 20:6: "Domine Deus audi clamorem hujus populi, et operi eis thesauram tuum fontem aquae vivae, ut satiati, cesset murmuratio eorum." (O Lord God, hear the cry of this people, and open to them thy treasure, a fountain of living water, that being satisfied, they may cease to murmur. Douay version.)

38. Exodus 15:23–25. See Daniélou, *Shadows to Reality*, p. 171.

39. MS. Bodl. 270b, Folio 50.

40. It is worth noting that the bronze serpent need only be looked on to heal, while the rods are to be kissed. I am reminded of the frequent occurrence of osculation in the liturgy.

41. Regrediente Dauid occurrerunt ei diuersis morborum generibus oppressi, qui uirtute sanctae crucis saluabantur" ("Geschichte," p. 142).

42. Regredienti David occurrerunt leprosi aridi ceci claudi diversis miseriis oppressi" (*Denkmäler Provenzalischer Literatur*, p. 186).

43. See, for example, Napier's comparison, *Holy Rood-tree*, p. xxxvii.

44. For the Middle Ages, David was at once a type of Christ, an Orphic poet, and exemplary of the ideal ruler. An illuminating study of the complex treatment of David in art is Hugo Steger, *David, rex et propheta: König David als vorbildliche Verkörperung des Herrschers und Dichters im Mittelalter, nach Bilddarstellungen des achten bis zwölften Jarhunderts* (Nuremberg, 1961).

45. *Quest*, p. 59.

46. See Suchier, *Denkmäler Provenzalischer Literatur*, p. 193; Meyer, *Geschichte*, p. 145.

47. Douay version. Compare *virgula* (a column of smoke) here with the *virgulae* (rods) of the legend.

48. *Rationale Divinorum Officiorum*, I, i.

49. A strong exegetical tradition, in fact, sees the litter as itself a type of the church: thus Isidore of Seville, "Ferculum Salomonis est sancta Ecclesia, quae credentes ad aeternae beatitudinis epulas levat, quae de fortibus animo, quasi de ligni imputribilibus, constructa est" (The litter of Solomon is the holy Church, which raises those who believe to feasts of everlasting felicity, and which is built of men strong in soul, as of wood that does not decay). *Expositio in Canticum Canticorum Salomonis* (*PL*, XXXIII, 1122). See also Alcuin, *Compendium in Cant. Cant.* (*PL*, C, 650). The variety of allegorical juggling acts is problematical here, however, since Solomon is himself a type of the church (Augustine, *PL*, XXXVII, 1668; Isidore, *PL*, LXXXIII, 113; Rabanus Maurus, *PL*, CIX, 186). St. Bernard seems to attempt a resolution of these multiplying symbols when he describes the cross, perhaps with this passage in mind, as "sedes sponsalis in qua Christus Ecclesiam sibi copulavit" (the betrothal seat upon which Christ united the Church with himself). *PL*, CLXXIV, 656. See the discussion of iconographic implications of these ideas in Adolf Katzenellenbogen, *The Sculptural Programs of Chartres Cathedral* (Baltimore, 1959), p. 15.

50. See Napier, *Holy Rood-tree*, p. 26.

51. See Reinhold Köhler, *Kleinere Schriften*, II, 87–94, and Jeanne Lucien Herr, "La Reine de Saba et le bois de la croix," *Révue Archéologique*, 4th series, 23 (1914): 1–31.

52. *Quest*, p. 55.

53. Auerbach remarks that "im hohen Mittelalter werden die Sybille, Vergil und die Gestalten der Aeneis, ja sogar Personen aus dem bretonischen Sagenkreise . . . in die figurale Deutung einbezogen, und es entstehen die mannigfachsten Kreuzungen aus figuralen, allegorischen und symbolischen Formen" (In the high Middle Ages the Sybil, Vergil, the figures of the *Aeneid*, and even characters from the Breton epic cycle . . . were included in the figural interpretation, and there result quite diverse crossings of figurative, allegorical, and symbolic forms). "Figura," *Archivum Romanicum*, 22 (1938): 478.

54. Quinn, however, thinks the name is taken from a Montanist prophetess. *Quest*, p. 129.

55. See M. Gaster, *Ilchester Lectures on Greeko-Slavonic Literature* (London, 1887), p. 36.

56. See Napier, *Holy Rood-tree*, p. 26.

57. In MS. Bodl. 600. See also H. H. Hilton, Jr., ed., "Seth, an Anglo-Norman Poem," *Studies in the Romance Languages and Literatures*, 2 (1941): 55.

58. In an unedited Italian poem cited by Adolfo Mussafia, "Sulla leggenda del legno della Croce," in *Sitzungsberichte der philosophisch-*

historischen Classe der kaiserlichen Akademie der Wissenschaften, 63 (1869): 188.

59. *Quest,* p. 60.

60. The later Cornish miracle fragment, the *Creation of the World,* does, to be sure, follow the *Ordinalia* in taking over part of the legend, but I know of no other.

61. Rahner, *Greek Myths,* p. 65.

62. Waldo F. McNeir, "The Corpus Christi Passion Plays as Dramatic Art," *Studies in Philology,* 48 (1951): 602.

63. After *RD* 1586: "sic finitur resurreccio domini . . . et incipit morte pilati." After *RD* 2360: "sic finitur mors pilati . . . et incipit ascencio Xti."

64. *Apocryphal New Testament,* pp. 157–158.

65. Chapter 53.

66. IV, iv (in London Rolls Series 41, ed. Churchill Babington and Joseph Rawson Lumby, 9 vols., 1865–1886).

67. See, for example, William Henry Hulme, ed., *The Middle-English Harrowing of Hell and Gospel of Nicodemus* (London: EETS, 1907). Paul Edward Kretzmann, *The Liturgical Element in the Earliest Forms of the Medieval Drama* (Minneapolis: University of Minnesota Studies in Language and Literature, 1916), p. 132, affirms that "in the Cornish Drama . . . the entire structure, as well as the subject matter, makes it evident that the Gospel of Nicodemus was the source of the [Harrowing of Hell] play."

68. Rose Jeffries Peebles, *The Legend of Longinus in Ecclesiastical Tradition and in English Literature, and Its Connection with the Grail* (Baltimore, 1911), pp. 131–141.

69. Jean Gray Wright, *A Study of the Themes of the Resurrection in the Mediaeval French Drama* (Bryn Mawr, Pa., 1935), pp. 20–21.

70. Ed. Foster, I, 168–173; ed. Heuser and Foster, pp. 34–36.

71. See Hadassah Posey Goodman, *Original Elements in the French and German Passion Plays: a Study of the Passion Scenes* (Bryn Mawr, Pa., 1944), pp. 53–55. Grace Frank, *The Medieval French Drama* (Oxford and New York, 1954), p. 127, points out that the incident occurs, perhaps originally, in the *Passion des Jongleurs,* but her assertion that the *Passion du Palatinus* "brings [the incident] upon the stage, probably for the first time," is questionable, since the Cornish plays may be older.

72. See M. D. Anderson, *Drama and Imagery in English Medieval Churches* (Cambridge, Eng., 1963), p. 106, and Mâle, *L'Art religieux de la fin du moyen âge,* p. 62.

73. See Rossell Hope Robbins and John L. Cutler, *Supplement to the Index of Middle English Verse* (Lexington, Ky., 1965), entry 158.3.

74. McNeir charitably suggests that it may serve as a "relief from the tension and strain of tragedy." "Corpus Christi Plays," p. 623.

75. See Réau, *Iconographie*, III, 1269.

76. This departing commission in the play appears to be based largely on the late addition to the conclusion of Mark (16:15–16), although the formula "hag yn weth why dew ha dew" (and also [go] you, two and two: *RD* 2463) apparently draws on a mission that is described biblically much earlier, in Mark 6:7. Thomas is especially commended to India.

77. In the Sarum rite this text forms the first lesson on the fourth day of Holy Week, and Carolus Marbach, ed., *Carmina Scripturarum* (Strasbourg, 1907), notes that it is used in antiphons at matins on the Feast of the Five Wounds and at vespers on the Feast of the Most Precious Blood.

78. T. H. Passmore, tr., *The Sacred Vestments: an English Rendering of the Third Book of the 'Rationale Divinorum Officiorum' of Durandus, Bishop of Mende* (London, 1899), p. 140.

79. In the *Stanzaic Life of Christ* it is called the *mundo sanguinio* (world of blood), and "the blody world of synne" (lines 8964, 8979).

80. See Daniélou, *Shadows to Reality*, p. 234.

81. Wilbur Gaffney, "The Allegory of the Christ-Knight in *Piers Plowman*," PMLA, 46 (1931): 167–168, points out the use of this theme in the Towneley Crucifixion and in the York Winedrawer's Play. Rosemary Woolf, "Doctrinal Influences on *The Dream of the Rood*," *Medium Aevum*, 27 (1958): 144, regards this idea as less prevalent than the view of Christ as a chivalric knight was to become.

82. *Legends of the Holy Rood*, p. 195.

83. *De Sacramentis Christianae Fidei* (*PL*, CLXXVI, 183), tr. Smalley, *Study of the Bible*, p. 89.

4. The Ordinalia and Doctrine

1. Gilbert, *Parochial History*, IV, 191–192.

2. "An Address on Religious Instruction," in Edward Rochie Hardy, ed., *Christology of the Later Fathers* (Philadelphia, 1954), p. 294.

3. "Religious Instruction," p. 301.

4. *A Commentary on the Apostles' Creed*, tr. J. N. D. Kelly (Westminster, Md., and London, 1955), p. 51.

5. In his sermon on the miracle of the five loaves and two fishes (130, ii): "Sed venit Redemptor, et victus est deceptor. Et quid fecit Redemptor noster captivatori nostro? Ad pretium nostrum tetendit muscipulam crucem suam; posuit ibi quasi escam sanguinem suum." (The Redeemer came, and the beguiler was overcome. And what did our Redeemer do to our capturer? For our ransom he set out his cross as a mouse trap, and there he placed his blood as the bait.) *PL,* XXXVIII, 726.

6. "Religious Instruction," pp. 300–302.

7. *Cur Deus Homo,* tr. James Gardiner Vose, ed. Sidney Norton Deane (LaSalle, Ill., 1951), vii, p. 188. This argument is given to Boso, Anselm's partner in the dialogue.

8. See the excellent treatment of Anselm's argument by R. W. Southern, *Saint Anselm and His Biographer* (Cambridge, Eng., 1963), pp. 77–121, and especially his synopsis, pp. 92–93. Of more thorough studies, those by René Roques, in the introduction to his edition of the text, *Pourquoi Dieu s'est fait homme* (Paris, 1963), and John McIntyre, *Saint Anselm and His Critics: A Reinterpretation of the 'Cur Deus Homo'* (Edinburgh, 1954), are particularly noteworthy.

9. "Sic ergo debet omnis qui peccat, honorem Deo quem rapuit solvere" (Therefore anyone who sins ought to repay God the honor that he has usurped). I, xi.

10. Roques, *Pourquoi Dieu,* introduction, p. 190. George H. Williams, "The Sacramental Presuppositions of Anselm's *Cur Deus Homo,*" *Church History,* 26 (1957): 245–274, argues that Anselm's "theory of the atonement was a rationalization of his eucharistic experience and practice" (p. 274n)—that, in other words, his ideas should be seen primarily as a reflection of the shift in sacramental emphasis from baptism to the eucharist.

11. R. W. Southern, *The Making of the Middle Ages* (New Haven, 1961), p. 236.

12. "Habemus in Francia novum de veteri magistro theologum, qui ab ineunte aetate sua in arte dialectica lusit, et nunc in Scripturis sanctis insanit." *Epistola 190, contra quaedam capitula errorum Abaelardi,* i (*PL,* CLXXXII, 1055). The letter is translated by Ailbe J. Luddy, *The Case of Peter Abelard* (Dublin, 1947), pp. 58–94.

13. The date seems acceptable, although some scholars have questioned it. See the discussion by J. G. Sikes, *Peter Abailard* (Cambridge, Eng., 1932), pp. 229–231.

14. Ailbe J. Luddy, *Life and Teaching of Saint Bernard* (Dublin, 1927), p. 413. William's argument is to be found in his *Disputatio adversus Petrum Abaelardum,* vii (*PL,* CLXXX, 269–276).

15. See Sikes, *Peter Abailard,* p. 187.

16. *Expositio in Epistolam ad Romanos,* II (*PL,* CLXXVIII, 834).

17. *PL,* CLXXVIII, 836.

18. "Quidquid horum sentiat, patet quantum humanae sacramento salutis invideat; quantum, quod in ipso est, evacuet alti dispensationem mysterii, qui totum de salute tribuit devotioni, regenerationi nihil: qui nostrae gloriam redemptionis, et summam salutis, non in virtute crucis, non in pretio sanguinis, sed in nostrae constituit conversationis profectibus." *PL,* CLXXXII, 1071–1072. Tr. by Luddy, *Case,* p. 92.

19. "Si omne quod profuit Christus, in sola fuit ostensione virtutum; restat ut dicatur, quod Adam quoque ex sola peccati ostensione nocuerit." *PL,* CLXXXII, 1071. Tr. by Luddy, *Case,* p. 90.

20. "Incomparabilis doctor, qui etiam profunda Dei sibi aperiens et ea quibus vult lucida et pervia faciens, altissimum sacramentum, et mysterium absconditum a saeculis, sic nobis suo mendacio planum et apertum reddit, ut transire leviter per illud possit quivis, etiam incircumcisus et immundus." *PL,* CLXXXII, 1067. Tr. by Luddy, *Case,* p. 83. Etienne Gilson, *The Philosophy of St. Bonaventure,* tr. Illtyd Trethowan and F. J. Sheed (New York, 1938), p. 487, perceptively draws attention to this fundamental difference in outlook between the disputants.

21. "Sequi [Jesum], salubre consilium; tenere et amplecti, solemne gaudium; manducare, vita beata . . . Ergo nec humilitatis exempla, nec charitatis insignia, praeter redemptionis sacramentum, sunt aliquid." *PL,* CLXXXII, 1072. Tr. by Luddy, *Case,* p. 93.

22. "Ei fortasse is praestat, per quem in terra oblivionis, gravedinis, lapsus nostri, tot et tantis gravaminibus Reparatoris fortius et vivacius admoneremur." *PL,* CLXXXII, 1069. Tr. by Luddy, *Case,* p. 86.

23. Etienne Gilson, *The Mystical Theology of Saint Bernard,* tr. A. H. C. Downes (London, 1940), p. 166, observes that the early twelfth century produced three great doctrines of love, in the work of Bernard, Abelard, and William of St. Thierry.

24. Gilson, *Mystical Theology,* p. 163.

25. References are to the translation of Aquinas' *Summa Theologica* by Fathers of the English Dominican Province (New York and elsewhere, 1947); Aquinas addresses himself to the efficacy of the redemption in II, iii, questions 46–48.

26. *Summa Theologica,* II, iii, q. 48 [4].

27. *Summa Theologica,* II, iii, q. 48 [6].

28. See notably the excellent studies of the idea by Jean Rivière: *Le Dogme de la Rédemption: Essai d'étude historique* (Paris, 1905), *Le Dogme de la Rédemption chez Saint Augustin* (Paris, 1928), *Le Dogme de la Rédemption après Saint Augustin* (Paris, 1930), *Le Dogme de la Rédemption: Etudes critiques et documents* (Louvain, 1931), and particularly *Le Dogme de la Rédemption au début du moyen age* (Paris, 1934), together with "Le Dogme de la Rédemption au XIIe siècle d'après les dernières publications," *Revue du Moyen Age latin,* 2 (1946): 101–112, 219–230, and the excellent summary article in the *Dictionnaire de théologie catholique,* XIII (Paris, 1936), s.v. *rédemption.* Also of interest are Hastings Rashdall, *The Idea of Atonement in Christian Theology* (London, 1919); L. W. Grensted, *A Short History of the Doctrine of the Atonement* (Manchester, 1920); Robert S. Franks, *The Atonement* (London, 1934) and *A History of the Doctrine of the Work of Christ in Its Ecclesiastical Development,* 2nd ed. (Edinburgh, 1962); H. E. W. Turner, *The Patristic Doctrine of Redemption* (London, 1952); and the provocative though aggressively Protestant essay by Gustav Aulén, *Christus Victor: An Historical Study of the Three Main Types of the Idea of Atonement,* tr. A. G. Hebert (New York, 1951).

29. "The Unity of the *Ludus Coventriae,*" *Studies in Philology,* 48 (1951): 529.

30. *PC* 1907f.

31. D. E. de Clerck, "Droits du démon et nécessité de la Rédemption: les écoles d'Abélard et de Pierre Lombard," *Recherches de Théologie ancienne et médiévale,* 14 (1947): 32–64, points out the general tendency among twelfth century thinkers to replace the difficult concept of the devil's rights with the somewhat equivocal notion of the devil's power.

32. Norris' translation of these lines—"that is true, he could destroy everything again that it be no more" (reading *moy ys na Je*)— seems preferable to Nance's emendation: "that is true: He could unmake all things again so that greater ease there could not be" (reading *moy es na ve*). Yet the notion is about the same in either case.

33. See *RD* 1476f.

34. The matter was, so to speak, in the air, and there is no evidence that the dramatist actually read Anselm, although it is worth remarking that he uses a phrase so curiously reminiscent of Anselm as the "honor of God" (*yn onour dev: OM* 1169, 1190, 1201, 1204). Noah and his family, immediately after the flood, erect an altar and make a sacrifice *yn dewellens pecadow* (in atonement of sins: *OM* 1173) atop Mount Calvary (*OM* 1180)—*yn onour dev.* This interesting phrase. Latinate as it is and used in the context of a typological allusion to the later sacrifice at the crucifixion, is not, to be sure, peculiarly Anselm's, but may be said to have an Anselmian flavor.

35. See, for example, *PC* 2172–2174.

36. See, for example, *PC* 234, 237, 241, 254, 289–290, 293, and 297 for the *pueri hebreorum;* and *PC* 665–666, where the apostle John makes just such an affirmation. When the three cripples are healed, they proclaim themselves in similar terms: as one of them remarks to Jesus,

> ro thy'm ow kerth dre the ras
> ha venytha me a grys

the vos a werghes genys
map dev agan dysprynnyas.

(Give me my walking, by thy grace; and hereafter I will believe thee to be born of a virgin, son of God, our Redeemer: *PC* 401–404.) For the assertion of Longinus, see *PC* 3025; of the centurion, *PC* 3079–3098.

37. See, for example, *PC* 364–366, 381–384, 1307–1320, 1696–1698, 2439–2444. James A. Devereux, S.J., has kindly pointed out to me that the speech is based on the biblical statement by Caiaphas that "it is expedient for us, that one man should die for the people, and that the whole nation perish not" (John 11:50).

38. Henry Jenner, in "The Cornish Drama," pp. 93–94, notes the popularity of the emblem of the mermaid in Cornish churches, where it frequently appears, for example, in bench-end carvings. Although Jenner observes that "the councils of Ephesus and Chalcedon might have found some fault with the advocate's way of expressing" the idea of the two natures of Christ in so bizarre an image, it is interesting to recall that William of Occam in the second quarter of the fourteenth century could speculate on whether God might as easily have become incarnate in an ass as a man: "Item: non includit contradictionem Deum assumere naturam asinam; igitur Deus illud potest facere" (Moreover, it does not involve a contradiction for God to take upon himself the nature of an ass: therefore it is possible for God to do so). *Centiloquium theologicum,* VI-A, in Philotheus Boehner, ed., *Franciscan Studies.* XXII, ii (June 1941), 44. Occam's rhetorical *asinus*-christology is, as Heiko Oberman has pointed out in *The Harvest of Medieval Theology: Gabriel Biel and Late Medieval Nominalism* (Cambridge, Mass., 1963), pp. 251f, directed at the nominalist question of the conceivability of the incarnation's taking place in an irrational being, whereas the dramatist's scholar with his mermaid is wondering if the incarnation could take place at all; yet both are concerned with the problem of the two natures of Christ. The mermaid is usually regarded, as Réau, *Iconographie,* I, 121, indicates, "comme le symbole de la Tentation diabolique par la Luxure" (as the symbol of diabolical temptation through lust), which probably explains its use in misericords and bench-end carvings, but makes all the more remarkable its function in the *Ordinalia.*

39. This interest is also present, one may note in passing, in the treatment of the prefigurative episode of Abraham's sacrifice. God uses the language of compulsion: "Thy son Isaac, whom thou lovest: it is necessary for thee to offer him" (*the vap ysac a geryth / y offrynne reys yv thy's: OM* 1279–1280). The incident is, of course, a test of Abraham's obedience.

40. See M. Salvina Westra, ed., *A Talkyng of þe Loue of God*

(The Hague, 1950). Though printed from a fourteenth century manuscript, this work is based on two thirteenth century treatises. Its spirit is certainly appropriate to the fourteenth century, however: "A swete Ihesu / swete lef. my deore herte. my lyues loue. Mi lyf. Mi deþ. Mi blisse. = For þou ordeyndest me. to þi deore lemmon. Bi twene þin armes ley I. me. Bi twene myn Armes cluppe I. þe" (p. 68).

41. Arthur Burkhard, "The Isenheim Altar," *Speculum*, 9 (1934): 59, says about this part of the remarkable work that "the Saviour has disappeared, the suffering martyr remains."

42. W. A. Pantin, *The English Church in the Fourteenth Century* (Cambridge, Eng., 1955), p. 243.

43. *Studies in Philology*, 48: 527–570.

44. *Piers Plowman and Contemporary Religious Thought* (London, n.d.), p. 125.

45. *Piers Plowman and the Scheme of Salvation: An Interpretation of 'Dowel, Dobet, and Dobest'* (New Haven, 1957), pp. 81–82, 86–94.

46. Citations in the text are to Walter W. Skeat, ed., *The Vision of William Concerning Piers the Plowman, in Three Parallel Texts, together with Richard the Redeless*, 2 vols. (Oxford, 1886).

47. The Latin allusion is apparently to Psalms 7:16 (Vulgate) /15 (King James): "et incidit in foveam quam fecit," "[He made a pit, and digged it,] and is fallen into the ditch which he made."

48. An interesting study, in this regard, is the doctoral dissertation by Stephen Joseph Laut, "Drama Illustrating Dogma: A Study of the York Cycle" (The University of North Carolina, 1960).

5. The Ordinalia and the Liturgy

1. Joseph A. Jungmann, *The Mass of the Roman Rite: Its Origins and Development*, tr. Francis A. Brunner (New York and elsewhere, 1951), I, 87f, points out the origins of the allegorical reading of the liturgy in the sixth century with Pseudo-Dionysius, although more specifically, in the Roman rite, with Alcuin and his pupil Amalarius of Metz in the ninth century.

2. Jungmann, I, 109.

3. *Rationale divinorum officiorum*, IV, i, 11. Although the popularity of Durandus' work is attested by an astonishing number of editions in the century after the invention of printing, the scholar today can unfortunately rely on nothing more recent than an edition published at Naples in 1859, edited by V. d'Avino.

4. Many of these texts have been assembled and are discussed by Karl Young, *The Drama of the Medieval Church*, 2 vols. (Oxford, 1933). O. B. Hardison, Jr., *Christian Rite and Christian Drama in* *the Middle Ages: Essays in the Origin and Early History of Modern Drama* (Baltimore, 1965), attempts to unravel the relationship between the forms of worship and of drama. Cf. Oscar Cargill, *Drama and Liturgy* (New York, 1930).

5. Cf. M. C. A. Sepet, *Les Prophètes du Christ: étude sur les origines du théâtre au moyen âge* (Paris, 1867–1868).

6. Hardin Craig, "The Origin of the Old Testament Plays," *Modern Philology,* 10 (1912–13): 473–487; and Kretzmann, *The Liturgical Element,* esp. pp. 76–88.

7. *Glossarium mediae et infimae latinitatis,* new ed., 10 vols. (Paris, 1937–1938).

8. Walter Howard Frere, *The Use of Sarum* (Cambridge, Eng., 1898), I, xii.

9. *Survey of Cornwall,* p. 145.

10. Henry Jenner discovered a Cornish fragment on the back of a fourteenth century charter in the British Museum and suggested that it might be part of such a promptbook, but it seems to be rather a jocular poem on marriage. See "The Fourteenth-Century Charter Endorsement, Brit. Mus. Add. Ch. 19491," *Journal of the Royal Institution of Cornwall,* 20 (1915): 41–48. The fragment was first printed by Whitley Stokes, "Cornica," *Revue celtique,* 4 (1878–81): 258–264, and has recently been printed and analyzed by Enrico Campanile, "Un Frammento scenico medio-cornico," *Studi e saggi linguistici* (supplement to *L'Italia Dialettale,* vol. 26), 3 (1963): 60–80.

11. Psalms 1.

12. Jenner, "Cornish Drama," p. 105.

13. See Legg, ed., *The Sarum Missal,* pp. 135, 141, 144, 145n4, 146, 149.

14. J. N. Dalton, ed., *Ordinale Exon.,* I (London: Henry Bradshaw Society, 1909), 138–139.

15. See Walter Howard Frere, *A Collection of His Papers on Liturgical and Historical Subjects* (London, 1940), pp. 54–71.

16. It was used as the introit for these masses in the Sarum rite, for example, from the Purification to the beginning of Advent. See Legg, ed., *The Sarum Missal,* p. 389. Several other hymns sharing this tag survive, but none was so well known as Sedulius'. It is, in fact, unusual for an introit chant to be based on a non-scriptural text—see Jungmann, *The Mass of the Roman Rite,* I, 321–330—and the Mass of the Virgin was particularly popular throughout the Middle Ages. For other hymns, see Hermann Adalbert Daniel, *Thesaurus Hymnologicus* (Leipzig, 1855–1856), V, 132, where a sequence of this title is listed; Guido Maria Dreves, *Analecta Hymnica Medii Aevi,* XXXII (Leipzig, 1899), 197–198; and Ulysse Chevalier, *Repertorium Hymnologicum*

(Louvain, 1892–1912; Brussels, 1920–21), II, 522–523, and III, 558.

17. *Paschalis carminis,* II, 63f, ed. Johannes Huemer in *Corpus Scriptorum Ecclesiasticorum Latinorum* (Vienna, 1866 et seq.), X, 48.

18. See Jungmann's excellent study of this hymn in *Mass of the Roman Rite,* I, 346–359.

19. See, for example, Frere, *Collection,* p. 65.

20. See Legg, ed., *Sarum Missal,* p. 94.

21. See "Cornish Drama," p. 88.

22. See Henry John Feasey, *Ancient English Holy Week Ceremonial* (London, 1897), pp. 76–77, and the discussion by John Walton Tyrer, *Historical Survey of Holy Week: Its Services and Ceremonial* (London, 1932), pp. 58–59, based on W. G. Henderson, ed., *Processionale ad usum insignis ac praeclarae ecclesiae Sarum* (Leeds, 1882), pp. 50–52.

23. *Drama of the Medieval Church,* I, 94.

24. E. Catherine Dunn, "Lyrical Form and the Prophetic Principle in the Towneley Plays," *Mediaeval Studies,* 23 (1961): 80.

25. See, for example, Henry Holland Carter, *A Dictionary of Middle English Musical Terms* (Bloomington, Ind., 1961).

26. *Music in the Middle Ages* (New York, 1940), p. 392.

27. *Chevalier* (I, 239) records a hymn, "crucifige! clamitant hora tertiarum."

28. A review in *Speculum,* 36 (1961): 695.

29. Ciprian Vagaggini, *Theological Dimensions of the Liturgy,* tr. L. J. Doyle (Collegeville, Minn., 1959), p. 135.

30. See Craig, "Origin of the Old Testament Plays," and Kretzmann, *The Liturgical Element,* pp. 76–88.

31. See, for example, the discussion of these several occasions by Prosper Guéranger, *L'Année liturgique* (Paris and elsewhere, 1868–1907), IV: *Le Temps de la septuagésime.*

32. See C. Callewaert, "L'Oeuvre liturgique de S. Grégoire: la Septuagésime et l'alleluia," *Revue d'histoire ecclésiastique,* 33 (1937): 306–326. Quadragesima, or Lent, is, as its name suggests, a season of forty days. The Sundays preceding this season are apparently—though inaccurately—denominated by analogy with it.

33. Solomon appears in the epistle read on Monday of the fourth week in Lent (1 Kings [Vulgate, 3 Kings] 3:16–28). See Guéranger, V: *Le Carême,* pp. 390–392. The incident in this reading is, however, unconnected with anything in the *Ordinalia.*

34. The Cornish name for the day is *De-Yow Hablys* (*PC* 654), apparently, like the Welsh *cablyd,* from Low Latin *capillatio:* the day, that is, on which monks were tonsured. See Nance, *Cornish-English Dictionary,* s.v. *cablys;* and R. J. Thomas, ed., *Geiriadur Prifysgol*

Cymru: A Dictionary of the Welsh Language (Cardiff, 1950 et seq.),
s.v. *cablyd*. Robert A. Fowkes has suggested to me that the words may
have entered the Brythonic languages by way of the Irish.

35. *The Liturgical Element*, p. 133; see also pp. 116–133.

36. Kretzmann, p. 121, reconstructs a liturgical type of dramatic
dialogue based on the antiphon:

> OFFICIATOR: Tollite portas, principes vestras, et elevamini,
>   portae eternales.
> CHORUS: Et introibit rex gloriae.
> DIACONUS (in figura diaboli): Quis est iste rex gloriae?
> CHORUS: Dominus virtutum ipse rex gloriae (fortis et potens).

By way of comparison, the Cornish version is clearly mimetic of such
a responsory:

> SPIRITUS CHRISTI: why pryncys a'n dewolow
>   scon egereugh an porthow
>
>   . . . .
>
>   sur may thello aberueth
>   an myghtern a lowene.
> LUCIFER: . . . Pyv myghtern a lowene . . .
> SPIRITUS: Arluth cref ha galosek
>   hag yn bateyl barthesek.

(Ye princes of the devils, immediately open the gates . . . surely that
the King of Joy may enter in. *Lucifer:* . . . . Who is the King of Joy?
. . . *Spiritus:* The Lord, strong and powerful, and valiant in battle:
RD 97–98, 103–104, 106, 108–109.)

37. See Tyrer, *Holy Week*, pp. 147f.

38. Tyrer notes (pp. 167–168) that this direction applied both in
the Sarum and York rites. André Lagarde, *The Latin Church in the
Middle Ages*, tr. Archibald Alexander (New York, 1915), deals briefly
with the historical change, pp. 35–37. See also L. Duchesne, *Christian
Worship: Its Origin and Evolution*, tr. M. L. McClure, 4th ed. (London, 1912), pp. 292f, and J. Bellamy, "Baptême dans l'église latine
depuis le VIIIe siècle avant et après et le concile de Trente," in *Diction-
naire de théologie catholique*, s.v. *baptême*. J. D. C. Fisher, *Christian
Initiation: Baptism in the Medieval West* (London, 1965), particularly
illuminates this change in baptismal practice in his analysis of the
gradual separation of the rite into the three ritual acts of baptism,
confirmation, and first communion.

39. *De Sacramentis Christianae Fidei*, PL, CLXXVI, 454–455.
The translation is by Roy J. Deferrari, *On the Sacraments of the
Christian Faith* (Cambridge, Mass., 1951), pp. 295–296.

40. Per Lundberg, *La Typologie baptismale dans l'ancienne eglise*
(Uppsala, 1942), p. 228.

Epilogue

1. Thurstan C. Peter, *The Old Cornish Drama* (London, 1906), p. 3.

2. Hardison, for example, in *Christian Rite and Christian Drama,* has sought to solve the problem by finding the germ of the drama in the ritual structure of the Mass. Jerome Taylor, "The Dramatic Structure of the Middle English Corpus Christi, or Cycle, Plays," in Bernice Slote, ed., *Literature and Society* (Lincoln, Neb., 1964), pp. 175–186, has ingeniously proposed a basic similarity between the commemorative intentions of the Feast of Corpus Christi and the intentions of the cycles. Another recent study deserving of mention in this context is V. A. Kolve, *The Play Called Corpus Christi* (Stanford, Calif., 1966).

3. Emile Mâle, *L'Art religieux du XIIIe siècle en France,* 8th ed. (Paris, 1948), p. vii.

4. W. S. Lach-Szyrma, *A Church History of Cornwall and of the Diocese of Truro* (London and elsewhere, n.d.), p. 68.

5. John Mason Neale and Benjamin Webb, trs., *The Symbolism of Churches and Church Ornaments: A Translation of the First Book of the Rationale Divinorum Officiorum, Written by William Durandus, Sometime Bishop of Mende* (Leeds, 1843), p. 53.

6. From Harl. MS. 1944, printed by F. J. Furnivall, ed., *The Digby Plays* (London: EETS, 1896), p. xxiii. See the discussion of Rogers by F. M. Salter, *Mediaeval Drama in Chester* (Toronto, 1955), pp. 54–55.

Index

3 5282 00249 3727